D A T

D0821447

The Dynamic Internet:
How Technology, Users,
and Businesses Are
Transforming the Network

The Dynamic Internet:
How Technology, Users,
and Businesses Are
Transforming the Network

Christopher S. Yoo

The AEI Press

Publisher for the American Enterprise Institute

WASHINGTON, D.C.

Distributed by arrangement with the Rowman & Littlefield Publishing Group, 4501 Forbes Boulevard, Suite 200, Lanham, Maryland 20706. To order, call toll free 1-800-462-6420 or 1-717-794-3800. For all other inquiries, please contact AEI Press, 1150 Seventeenth Street, N.W., Washington, D.C. 20036, or call 1-800-862-5801.

Library of Congress Cataloging-in-Publication Data

Yoo, Christopher S.
  The dynamic internet : how technology, users, and businesses are changing the network / Christopher S. Yoo.
       p. cm.
  Includes bibliographical references and index.
  ISBN 978-0-8447-7227-1 (cloth)—ISBN 0-8447-7227-5 (cloth)—
  ISBN 978-0-8447-7229-5 (ebook)—ISBN 0-8447-7229-1 (ebook)
  1. Internet industry. 2. Business networks. 3. Internet industry—Prices.
I. Title.

  HD9696.8.A2Y66 2010
  384.3'3—dc23
                                                        2012015322

Printed in the United States of America

For my sons, Marshall and Brendan

Contents

List of Illustrations

TABLES

Acknowledgments

The author would like to thank the Milton and Miriam Handler Foundation, the New York Bar Foundation, the National Research Initiative, and the Center for Technology, Innovation and Competition at the University of Pennsylvania for their financial support.

The manuscript benefited from presentations at the Wharton Communication and Media Law Colloquium, the Princeton Center for Information Technology Policy, the Columbia University chapters of the Association for Computing Machinery (ACM) and Scientists and Engineers for a Better Society, the Penn Intellectual Property Group, the Earle Mack School of Law at Drexel University, and the Annenberg School for Communication.

The book draws on material from the following publications:

Yoo, Christopher S. 2008. Network neutrality, consumers, and innovation. *University of Chicago Legal Forum* (2008):169–262.

———. 2010. Free speech and the myth of the Internet as an unintermdiated experience. *George Washington Law Review* 78 (4): 697–773.

———. 2010. Innovations in the Internet's architecture that challenge the status quo. *Journal on Telecommunications and High Technology Law* 8 (1): 79–99.

———. 2010. Product life cycle and the maturation of the Internet. *Northwestern University Law Review* 104 (2): 641–70.

List of Acronyms

ADSL	asymmetric digital subscriber line
AOL	America Online
ARPANET	Advanced Research Projects Agency Network
BGP	Border Gateway Protocol
CAGR	compounded annual growth rate
CAN-SPAM	Controlling the Assault of Nonsolicited Pornography and Marketing (Act)
CDN	content delivery network
ConEx	congestion exposure
DARPA	Defense Advanced Research Projects Agency
DBS	direct broadcast satellite
DiffServ	differentiated services
DNS	domain name system
DOCSIS	Data Over Cable Service Interface Specification
DSL	digital subscriber line
DTC	(University of Minnesota's) Digital Technology Center
ECN	Explicit Congestion Notification
FCC	Federal Communications Commission
FIND	(NSF's) Future Internet Design
FiOS	(Verizon's) Fiber Optic Service
FTTH	fiber to the home
Gbps	gigabits per second
GENI	(NSF's) Global Environment for Network Innovations
IANA	Internet Assigned Numbers Authority
ICANN	Internet Corporation for Assigned Names and Numbers

IPv4	Internet Protocol version 4
ISP	Internet service provider
ITU	International Telecommunication Union
kbps	kilobits per second
LEDBAT	low extra-delay background transport
LTE	Long Term Evolution
Mbps	megabits per second
MPLS	MultiProtocol Label Switching
NAP	network access point
NewArch	(DARPA's) New Architecture
NSF	National Science Foundation
NSFNET	National Science Foundation Network
PC	personal computer
QoS	quality of service
RED	Random Early Discard
RFID	radio frequency identification
TCP	Transmission Control Protocol
UDP	User Datagram Protocol
URL	Uniform Resource Locator
VCR	videocassette recorder
VDSL	very high bit rate digital subscriber line
VoIP	voice over Internet Protocol
WiFi	Wireless Fidelity
WiMax	Worldwide Interoperability for Microwave Access

Introduction

When I took office [in January of 1993], only high energy physicists had ever heard of what is called the World Wide Web. Now even my cat has his own web page.

—William J. Clinton (1996)

The mid-1990s represented the seminal moment in the history of the Internet. Spurred by the invention of the World Wide Web in 1989, the launch of the first browser capable of supporting graphics in 1993, and the privatization of the Internet backbone in 1995 (and the accompanying removal of all restrictions on commercial use), the Internet ceased being the plaything of the high-tech community and started to become part of almost everyone's daily life. A medium that began as a way for academics to exchange e-mail and transfer files has now transformed virtually every aspect of most people's everyday lives, putting a previously unimaginable range of information at their fingertips and changing the way they work, play, learn, and vote.

Many policy advocates argue that the Internet of the mid-1990s was built around certain architectural principles that created a uniform, level playing field that provided everyone with nondiscriminatory access to the network. These advocates regard these principles as critical to the Internet's past success and have called on Congress and federal regulatory agencies to mandate that those principles remain in place (see, for example, Lessig 2006; FCC 2009).

Leading technologists have challenged the historical accuracy of these arguments, pointing out that they presuppose a golden age that never really existed (Crowcroft 2007; Clark 2008).[1] As the inclusion of a "type of service" flag in the original Internet Protocol header demonstrates, the ability to prioritize particular traffic based on its need for throughput, delay avoidance, and reliability has been one of the Internet's central design features from the very beginning. Moreover, because the Department of Defense's Advanced Research Projects Agency (DARPA) initially created the Internet to be a military network, it placed a high priority on considerations that have little relevance to commercial networks (such as survivability in the face of attack) and placed a low priority on considerations that are critical to a commercial network's success (such as efficiency and cost accountability) (Clark 1988).

Setting aside whether the above accurately describes the Internet when it first emerged as a mass-market phenomenon, the policy debate has largely overlooked the extent to which the technological and economic environments surrounding the Internet have changed since the mid-1990s. Specifically, four major changes that have forced the network to evolve remain underdiscussed:

1. *Increase in the number and diversity of end users*: What was once a small population of technologically savvy scientific researchers based in universities and research institutions has been replaced by a user base that is much larger, more diverse, and less technologically sophisticated and that receives less institutional support.

2. *Increase in the diversity and intensity of applications*: Early Internet applications, such as e-mail and file transfers, required relatively little bandwidth and were not particularly sensitive to variations in network performance. Modern applications, such as videoconferencing and online gaming, often demand greater bandwidth, security, and performance. Other applications, such

---

[1] Crowcroft notes, "The Internet was never really a level playing field....[T]he idea that the network is innately fair...is fairly bogus." Clark similarly observed that "the Internet is not neutral and has not been for a long time."

as peer-to-peer technologies and cloud computing, create traffic patterns that are fundamentally different from previous mass-market applications.

3. *Increase in the variety of technologies*: When the Internet first arose, almost everyone connected to it via a desktop computer that was attached to a connection provided by the local telephone company. Dial-up modems have now given way to a wide array of last-mile networking technologies, including cable modem systems, digital subscriber lines (DSL), fiber-to-the-home, and wireless broadband. In contrast to the relative uniformity of wireline connections, these new technologies vary widely in terms of their available bandwidth, reliability, mobility, and susceptibility to local congestion. The number of devices used to connect to the Internet has diversified as well and now includes laptops, smartphones, specialized devices (such as e-readers like the Amazon Kindle), and radio-frequency identification tags (best known to most consumers as the small electronic tags attached to merchandise to avoid shoplifting). Compared to desktop computers, these devices are much more sensitive to conflicts between applications as well as the amount of power that each application consumes. Moreover, they differ in their capacity to perform basic functions demanded by many Internet protocols, like sending acknowledgments for every packet received.

4. *The emergence of more complex business relationships*: The topology of the Internet began as a strict three-level hierarchy consisting of backbones, regional Internet service providers (ISPs), and last-mile providers (sometimes called tier 1, tier 2, and tier 3 providers). Over time, the networks comprising the Internet began to enter into a much more diverse set of business relationships, like private peering, multihoming, secondary peering, content delivery networks (CDNs), and server farms.

These changes are placing increasing pressure on the Internet to develop new architectural principles better suited to supporting the greater demands that end users are now placing on the network. The engineering literature is replete with laundry lists of functions that the Internet does not perform well, including mission-critical features such as security, mobility, quality of service; more efficient distribution of video; and the ability to support end users who maintain multiple connections (a practice known as *multihoming*) (Handley 2006; Crowcroft 2007; Spyropoulos, Fdida, and Kirkpatrick 2007; Ortiz 2008). The Internet Engineering Task Force (IETF), the primary standard-setting organization for the Internet, has approved standards for a wide range of sophisticated tools for network management.[2] Many scholars are pursuing a variety of "clean slate" initiatives that examine how the Internet's architecture might be different if it were designed from scratch today (Bellovin et al. 2005; Crowcroft and Key 2007; Feldmann 2007; Ortiz 2008; Banniza et al. 2009; International Center for Advanced Internet Research 2010; and Stanford University Clean Slate Project n.d.; and for cautionary notes, see Dovrolis 2008). Government agencies charged with promoting scientific research share the same concerns. DARPA and the National Science Foundation (NSF) have launched programs to explore alternative network architectures better suited to supporting end users' increasing demands for greater security and network management (Clark et al. 2003; NSF n.d.a, n.d.b, n.d.c). European governments are supporting similar initiatives (European Commission Directorate-General for the Information Society 2010; European Commission n.d.; Spyropoulos, Fdida, and Kirkpatrick 2007).

The dramatic shift in Internet usage suggests that its founding architectural principles from the mid-1990s may no longer be appropriate today. Restructuring the Internet to best fit today's usage requires consideration of the following seven elements:

1. *Changes in the optimal level of standardization*: Engineers and economists have long recognized that standardization creates

---

[2] These include integrated services (IntServ) (Braden et al. 1994); differentiated services (DiffServ) (Blake et al. 1998); MultiProtocol Label Switching (MPLS) (Rosen et al. 2001); and Explicit Congestion Notification (ECN) (Ramakrishnan et al. 2001). The IETF is currently evaluating other initiatives, including Low Extra Delay Back-ground Transport (LEDBAT) and Congestion Exposure (ConEx) (Shalunov et al. 2011; Mathis and Briscoe 2011).

both benefits and costs, with the optimal level of standardization determined by the relative uniformity or heterogeneity of what people want from the network. If costs are identical and what consumers want from the network is uniform, the optimal outcome is a single network optimized to provide the precise services that consumers want. As consumer demand and the technologies comprising the network become more heterogeneous, it eventually becomes preferable for the network protocols, topology, and business relationships to become more varied to meet end users' increasingly varied needs. Under these circumstances, the development of new Internet architectures may represent nothing more than the network's natural attempt to respond to changes in technology and user demand. Indeed, the emergence of such diversity becomes not so much a problem as an essential precondition for meeting consumer demands that are growing increasingly wide ranging.

2. *The shift toward more formal governance*: The Internet has long depended primarily on cooperative behavior and informal sanctions to ensure that the network functions effectively and that those using the network behave in a nondisruptive manner. The increase in the number and heterogeneity of end users will likely lead to increased reliance on more formal modes of governance.

3. *The migration of functions into the core of the network*: Scale economies, the need for centralized information about the actions of multiple users, and the growing distrust of other endpoints is causing certain functions, such as security and congestion management, to migrate from the edge of the network into its core.

4. *The growing complexity of Internet pricing*: When the Internet first emerged as a mass-market phenomenon in the mid-1990s, it was characterized by a fairly simple set of pricing relationships. Since that time, a number of forces, such as the increasing heterogeneity of end users' bandwidth consumption, the need to manage congestion, the need to finance bandwidth expansion,

the advent of peer-to-peer technologies, and the growing importance of advertising as a revenue source, are leading the industry toward a more diverse array of pricing arrangements.

5. *The inevitability of intermediation*: Many early commentators lauded the Internet's ability to bypass gatekeepers and allow speakers to connect directly with their audiences. The transformation of the Internet from a platform of person-to-person communications into the leading platform for mass communications has made intermediation inevitable—to screen out unwanted content, to facilitate access to desired content, and to take advantage of new architectural approaches to delivering content. Contrary to what some policy advocates have suggested, Supreme Court precedent confirms that such intermediation promotes rather than impedes free-speech values.

6. *Incomplete convergence and the myth of the one screen*: Many industry observers have long predicted the complete convergence of communications technologies, in which consumers receive all of their communications through a single connection. Other considerations suggest that end users will continue to maintain multiple network connections (that is, multihome), partly motivated by the desire to increase network reliability, to reduce cost, and to take advantage of key technological differences between technologies (such as mobility). The persistence of multihoming undercuts the need for every network connection to be everything to everyone. It also limits the potential for any network actor to act in an anticompetitive manner.

7. *The maturation of the industry*: Economists and management scholars have long studied how an industry's structure and the nature of competition evolve over time. These groups have advanced a wide range of models driven by different motivating considerations and surrounded by empirical studies both confirming and contradicting the theoretical results. Although further research is needed, the preliminary findings underscore that change over time is inevitable: it is not a question of *if* the network architecture will adjust but *how* and *when*.

Considering these seven elements of Internet usage and evolution, it becomes clear that the static, one-size-fits-all approach that dominates the current debate misses the mark. On the contrary, the architecture of the future is likely to be more dynamic and heterogeneous. The elements I have identified also underscore the fact that network engineering is a pragmatic, context-sensitive discipline that is an exercise in tradeoffs that is not susceptible to broad, theoretical generalizations.[3] As end users place increasingly intense and heterogeneous demands on the network, the natural response is for the network architecture to adapt to meet those needs by incorporating additional functionality and flexibility. Rather than offering end users a single uniform product, different portions of the network may respond in different ways, offering end users a variety of services from which to choose, a practice I have called *network diversity* (Yoo 2006). Such diversification can provide end users with services that better fit their needs while simultaneously making the industry more competitive. Equally important, the optimal network architecture is unlikely to be static. Instead, it is likely to be dynamic over time, changing with the shifts in end-user demands. In short, the network must evolve to meet the new demands being placed on it by an environment that is constantly changing.

Network engineering thus has a contingent and dynamic quality that does not lend itself to simple policy inferences or categorical statements about which architecture is inherently better. At the same time, past experience has taught that experts usually cannot anticipate which solutions will succeed and which will fail. Consider, for example, America Online's 2001 acquisition of Time Warner. While many critics warned that the merger might mark the end of the public Internet, in retrospect it simply marked the end of America Online (AOL) as a major industry player and the destruction of approximately $200 billion in shareholder value.

---

[3] A leading textbook on computer networking notes that "understanding network performance is more an art than a science. There is little underlying theory that is actually of any use in practice. The best we can do is give rules of thumb gained from hard experience and present examples taken from the real world" (Tanenbaum 2003). The pragmatism underlying network engineering is also reflected in David Clark's (1992) famous statement that "we believe in rough consensus and running code," as well as in the IETF's refusal to approve a standard until there are two independent implementations up and running.

The difficulty in determining in advance precisely what architectural vision will ultimately win out highlights the importance of what engineers call *designing for tussle* by creating policies that are flexible enough to permit experiments with different solutions as the technology, consumer needs, and business environment become ever more diverse and complex (Clark et al. 2005). The importance of providing the latitude to try new solutions that deviate from the status quo is reinforced by the literature on network economics, which suggests that networks may be characterized by too *little* change, not too *much* (David 1985; Farrell and Saloner 1985; Arthur 1989; Katz and Shapiro 1994). Technologists share the same concern, often commenting on the nearly insuperable obstacles that are preventing the Internet from evolving into a new architecture (Laskowski and Chuang 2009; Anderson et al. 2005; Crowcroft 2007; Ratnasamy, Shenker, and McCanne 2005; Martin 2007).

Just as engineers must design structures that preserve room for experimentation, so must regulators. In particular, regulators should avoid promulgating policies that foreclose certain technical approaches or require industry actors to obtain advance approval before they can experiment with new technological solutions. The benefits of most practices will remain ambiguous before they are deployed, and placing the burden on industry actors to prove consumer benefit before imple-mentation would chill experimentation and effectively prevent ambiguous practices from ever being deployed. This in turn would prevent engineers from obtaining the real-world experience they need to evaluate differ-ent technological solutions and eliminate the breathing room on which technological progress depends.

In the face of such uncertainty, policymakers should not attempt to predict which particular network solution will ultimately prevail; rather, they ought to focus on creating regulatory structures that give industry participants the freedom to pursue a wide range of business strategies and allow consumers to decide which one (or ones, if consumer demand is sufficiently diverse to support multiple business models targeted at different market niches) ultimately proves to be the best. The uncertainty surrounding the network's optimal configuration in the future provides further support for a regulatory approach inspired by the Supreme Court's antitrust jurisprudence, which examines particular practices on a case-by-case basis after they have been implemented and places the burden of proof on the party challenging the practice (Yoo 2004, 2005, 2006, 2008, 2009). Such an approach would preserve room for experimentation, while at the same time give regulators the authority to address any problems that might emerge.

Any such case-by-case approach should bear in mind Nobel Prize winner Ronald Coase's warning (1972) that "when an economist finds something—a business practice of one sort or another—that he does not understand, he looks for a monopoly explanation." Coase's point is that the fact that a business practice may be novel or disruptive should not necessarily lead to the presumption that it is necessarily harmful to consumers. Any change necessarily creates new winners and losers, which will inevitably prompt those disadvantaged by a change to argue that it is anticompetitive.

As a result, it is important to keep in mind that that change is often simply the natural response to changes in technology as well as shifts in what consumers are demanding from the network and the ways in which new technologies can satisfy those demands. Scholars of innovation generally regard experimentation and conflicts over standards as symptoms of economic and innovative health and emphasize that divided technical leadership and pressure on existing interfaces can represent an important form of competition (Bresnahan 1999; Greenstein 2010).

A more nuanced and technologically sophisticated perspective underscores how the types of changes we are witnessing can actually reduce costs and enhance network services in ways that benefit individual consumers and society as a whole. It also underscores the potential dangers of advocating simple, categorical solutions that adhere too closely to the status quo for its own sake in ways that effectively lock a particular technological conception of the Internet into place. While unruly, changes in the network's architecture are both inevitable and a natural part of the technological and social progress. Far from being regarded as a problem in need of remediation, change should be embraced as a natural and indispensable part of the process of the Internet's evolution.

Part I

Changes in the Technological and Economic Environment

1

Increases in the Number and Diversity of Internet Users

The universe of Internet users has undergone a fundamental transformation since the mid-1990s. The number of people using the Internet has become both larger and more diverse in terms of technological sophistication, institutional support, and shared values. At the same time, however, the period of rapid growth is beginning to slow down as the market begins to approach its saturation point.

Growth in the Number of Users and Computers Connected to the Internet

The Internet's growth can be measured either in terms of the number of *people* connected to it or in terms of the number of *computers* connected to it. Starting with the former approach, data collected by the International Telecommunication Union (ITU) indicate that the number of Internet users in the United States was extremely small prior to the mid-1990s. After that time, the number of U.S. Internet users climbed sharply until the end of the decade, after which point the growth curve began to level out. As of 2009, 240 million of the roughly 300 million people living in the United States were Internet users. Measured solely in terms of broadband connections, the U.S. subscribership has risen rapidly over the past decade. (Note in figure 1-1 that the number of broadband subscriptions understates the total number of broadband users, as a single subscription typically serves several users living in the same household.) Growth has begun to taper off during the last year, suggesting that the market may be beginning to approach saturation even within the broadband market.

FIGURE 1-1

U.S. INTERNET USERS AND BROADBAND SUBSCRIBERS (MILLIONS)

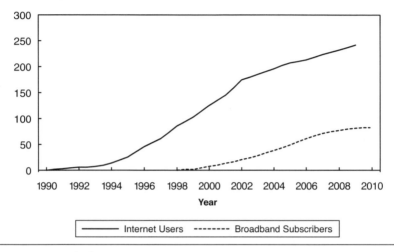

SOURCE: International Telecommunication Union (n.d.).

FIGURE 1-2

U.S. INTERNET USERS AND BROADBAND PENETRATION

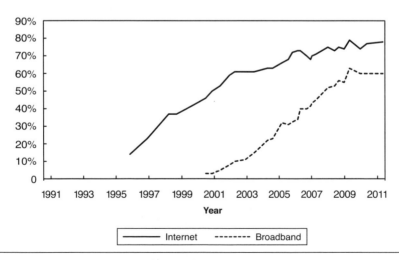

SOURCE: Pew Internet and American Life Project (n.d.).

Instead of counting subscribers, other institutions conduct surveys to measure the percentage of citizens that use the Internet (figure 1-2). The data produced by these surveys follow patterns similar to the ITU's subscribership data. Again, penetration rates were relatively low during the early 1990s, accelerating sharply during the mid-1990s. Growth in penetration rates began to slow during the early 2000s and has now reached 78 percent. The last decade has also witnessed a dramatic growth in broadband connections only to see the growth curve flatten as the market began to approach saturation. Data collected by Nielsen corroborate this conclusion (Internet World Stats 2010).

The Internet's growth can also be measured in terms of the number of computers connected to its edge—commonly called *hosts* (figure 1-3). Since the mid-1990s, the number of hosts connected to the Internet has exploded, increasing from just fewer than 6 million in January 1995 to nearly 850 million as of July 2011. Unlike the growth rates for end users, the growth rates for hosts do not yet appear to be tapering off.

FIGURE 1-3
GLOBAL INTERNET HOSTS (MILLIONS)

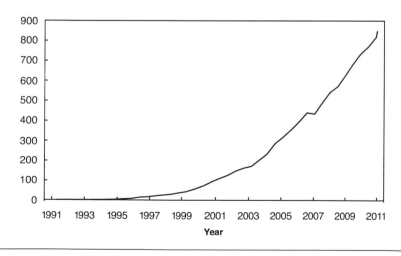

SOURCE: Internet Systems Consortium (2010).

This pattern of end-user growth carries with it a number of important implications for broadband policy that have been largely overlooked. As an initial matter, the total number of possible connections for n end points equals $n(n-1)/2$. This means that the number of possible connections increases with the square of the number of end users. The fact that the number of end users increases quadratically with the number of connections means that routing and network management will become increasingly difficult as the network grows. Furthermore, as discussed in greater detail in later chapters, the dramatic increase in the number and diversity of end users has implications for the optimal level of network standardization, the continuing ability to rely on informal modes of governance, and the complexity of pricing. In addition, the fact that market growth appears to be reaching saturation indicates that the nature of competition and innovation may be about to change in a fundamental way.

Changes in the Nature of Users

As noted earlier, when the Internet first arose, it was almost exclusively the province of academics based in large institutions conducting computer-oriented research. Even the first generation of users outside the academic community tended to speak of it as something precious and distinct from anything that had existed before.

The emergence of the Internet as a mass-market phenomenon has resulted in more than just an increased number of people using the network; it has also meant an entirely new kind of user. Specifically, Internet users have changed in the following ways:

- *Greater geographic dispersion*: The emergence of the Internet as a global phenomenon has caused the average distance between end points to increase. Since packets cannot travel faster than the speed of light, the increased distance necessarily means an increase in latency between endpoints that are relatively distant. It also puts upward pressure on the number of router hops that the average communication may need to traverse, which in turn complicates the management problem and introduces greater potential for delay.

- *Less technical sophistication*: As the Internet entered the main-stream, end users no longer consisted primarily of computer scientists who are relatively technologically savvy. Instead, the population of end users came to be comprised primarily of people without the technical training to solve the issues that arise from time to time. Many problems that the network could once expect end users to solve themselves must now be addressed with greater assistance from other actors.

- *Less institutional support*: The fact that end users are often in households instead of research institutions means that they are less likely to enjoy the support of information-technology staff dedicated to helping resolve their problems.

- *Fewer shared values*: The Internet's move outside the academic community also means that end users are likely to be much more heterogeneous in the way they use the network. Instead of using the Internet for e-mail, file transfers, and news-groups, mass-market users are more likely to use the Internet for commercial purposes that place far different demands on the network. Equally importantly, end users can no longer be expected to share a common set of values and professional experiences. Instead of consisting of colleagues educated in a similar manner and who have repeated professional contacts with one another, the population of end users is now likely to be far more diverse, atomized, and anonymous. As a result, the universe of end users has become less trustworthy, as reflected by the increased frequency of spam, viruses, invasions of privacy, and other forms of malicious behavior (Blumenthal and Clark 2001; Kempf and Austein 2004; Yoo 2004).

These massive user changes in turn affect what is expected from the network. The lack of technical sophistication and institutional support may lead end users to expect to be provided with services that were once performed by the first users themselves. In addition, the increase in end-user heterogeneity can be expected to increase the level of conflict between users, both because of the increasing diversity in what people want from the network and because of the erosion of the common set of values and experiences that used to unite the Internet community.

The emergence of the Internet as a mass-market phenomenon in turn places pressure on the Internet's architecture to change. As what people want from the network becomes increasingly varied, it is natural for the network to evolve in response. In addition, it should not be surprising that the cooperative ethos that characterized its early days has begun to be replaced by more formal means of governance.

2

Changes in the Nature of Internet Usage

In addition to the increase in the number and variety of end users connected to the Internet, the years since the mid-1990s have witnessed a fundamental shift in the nature and variety of the applications running on the Internet. The first "killer application" of the early Internet was e-mail, which accounted for as much as 75 percent of all traffic on the Advanced Research Projects Agency Network (ARPANET). Then in 1989 Tim Berners-Lee conceived of an architecture to integrate hypertext into the Internet. In 1993, Marc Andressen created the first graphics-oriented Web browser. Together these innovations laid the foundations for the other dominant application of the early Internet: the World Wide Web.

E-mail and Web browsing represented the two primary drivers for the first generation of the Internet's growth. Today, however, a new generation of applications is emerging, with leading examples including Internet Protocol television (IPTV), peer-to-peer file sharing, and cloud computing. These new applications are placing much greater demands on the network in terms of bandwidth and quality of service (QoS). They are also placing pressure on the network architecture to evolve in more fundamental ways.

Bandwidth Intensiveness

End users' demand for bandwidth has undergone a remarkable period of sustained growth. The University of Minnesota's Digital Technology Center (DTC) has long been collecting data on the volume of traffic passing through the network. Because of the uncertainty in the data, in 1997 DTC began reporting an upper estimate and lower estimate for Internet

FIGURE 2-1

GROWTH IN U.S. INTERNET TRAFFIC (PETABYTES/MONTH)

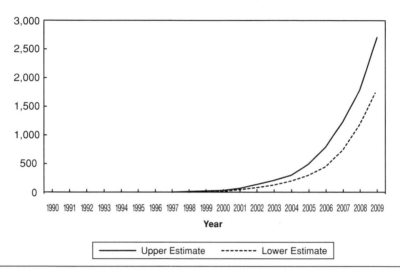

SOURCE: Minnesota Internet Traffic Studies (n.d.).

traffic rather than a single definitive number. These data indicate that the amount of traffic traveling over the Internet has grown at a compounded annual growth rate (CAGR) of between 118 percent and 123 percent for the past twenty years (figure 2-1).

A closer examination of the data reveals that bandwidth growth can be divided into two periods (figure 2-2). From 1990 to 2002 it grew at a rate of roughly 100 percent each year with the exception of two years (1995 and 1996), when Internet traffic grew at the incredible rates of 838 percent and 900 percent. Starting in 2003, Internet traffic growth slowed to an annual rate of between 50 percent and 60 percent (see also Cisco Systems 2010b).

The clear outliers are 1995 and 1996. What accounts for this nearly tenfold increase in the amount of traffic in just two short years? Although the number of end users and hosts increased during this time, the growth rates were not markedly different from earlier or later periods and thus are insufficient to explain a traffic increase of this magnitude.

FIGURE 2-2

ANNUAL GROWTH RATES FOR U.S. INTERNET TRAFFIC

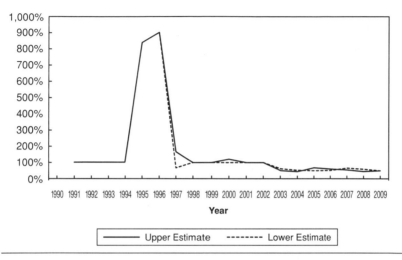

SOURCE: Minnesota Internet Traffic Studies (n.d.).

The explanation lies not in the number of people using the Internet but rather in the *applications* they were running. Simply put, the primary cause of this sharp increase in network usage was the arrival of the World Wide Web. Not only did the Web boost the amount of time end users spent online, it also increased the intensity of their usage. Prior to the release of the Mosaic browser in 1993, Internet traffic consisted almost exclusively of text, which requires relatively little bandwidth to convey. The Mosaic browser's graphical user interface increased the number of illustrations and photography flowing through the network, which greatly accelerated the demand for network capacity. The resulting spike turned the Internet into what many called the "World Wide Wait."

Many industry observers are concerned that the shift of video to Internet-based technologies will produce an "exaflood" that will once again cause growth rates to accelerate.[4] For example, a Cisco report projected

[4] The term *exaflood* is most commonly associated with George Gilder (Swanson and Gilder 2008). For similar observations, see Borland 2006, Norton 2006, Swanson 2007, Deloitte 2007, Nemertes Research 2007, Windhausen 2008, and Reuters 2007.

that Internet video would account for more than half of all global consumer Internet traffic by 2012. And if one includes all forms of video (conventional television, video on demand, and peer-to-peer), video would represent over 90 percent of all consumer bandwidth by that time (Cisco Systems 2010a and 2011b; *see also* Norton 2006). Indeed, if all of the video currently distributed via broadcasting and cable were to migrate to the Internet, the amount of bandwidth would far exceed the current capacity of the entire Internet (Minnesota Internet Traffic Studies n.d.).

These predictions have prompted a vigorous debate over the Internet's likely future (Delaney 2007). DTC, for example, sees no sign of a widescale exaflood. Others contest this conclusion, arguing that by only monitoring traffic passing through public peering points the DTC fails to take into account the growing proportion of traffic that bypasses through the public backbone. And even skeptics recognize that traffic on wireless broadband networks is growing at significantly faster rates: Cisco reports that wireless data traffic grew at a rate of over 150 percent between 2007 and 2010 and projects a growth rate of 92 percent between now and

TABLE 2-1

GROWTH IN INTERNATIONAL INTERNET TRAFFIC AND CAPACITY

	Average Traffic	Peak Traffic	International Bandwidth
2004	104%	105%	45%
2005	50%	57%	41%
2006	74%	57%	45%
2007	61%	63%	69%
2008	53%	58%	62%
2009	74%	79%	64%
2010	62%	56%	55%
2011	37%	53%	47%
CAGR	68%	68%	55%

SOURCES: TeleGeography Research 2007, 2008, 2009, 2010, 2011.

2015 (Cisco Systems 2009, 2010a, 2011a; see also Nemertes Research 2007; Minnesota Internet Traffic Studies 2009).

Other data collected by the market-research firm TeleGeography indicate a recent upturn in the demand for bandwidth (table 2-1). If this growth represents a permanent change, network providers will have to increase the rate at which they are adding capacity.

The emergence of these new, bandwidth-intensive applications has the potential to place extreme pressure on the network. Network providers must make contingency plans to accommodate a possible sudden surge in user traffic; unfortunately, the problem is that capacity increases are costly and cannot be done instantaneously, with last-mile networks facing greater costs and lead times than backbones and other providers operating in the core of the network. The ability to expand capacity is particularly limited for wireless broadband networks, with the amount of spectrum available placing a sharp limit on the wireless providers' ability to build bigger pipes (Odlyzko 2003; Cisco Systems 2008a).

Sensitivity to Jitter, Delay, and Unreliability

More bandwidth is only one type of enhanced service that video and other new applications are demanding from the network. The performance of traditional Internet applications, such as e-mail and Web browsing, depends almost exclusively on when the last packet in a particular Internet transmission arrives at its destination. Modern Internet applications, rather, are much more sensitive to the order and the timing with which intermediate packets arrive. In fact, engineering textbooks typically describe three other dimensions of quality of service that networks provide:

- *Reliability/Packet Loss*: A network is said to deliver high reliability when all of the packets arrive at the receiving host without any errors. The Transmission Control Protocol (TCP), which remains the workhorse of the Internet, employs a simple mechanism to ensure reliability. For every packet that arrives intact, the receiving host sends an acknowledgment back to the sending host. If the sending host fails to receive an acknowledgment within the expected time, it simply resends the packet.

- *Delay*: Also called latency, delay is the time it takes for an application to begin operating after a request for service has been placed. Delay can result from the distance that the packet needs to travel, from the amount of computer processing needed to determine a packet's from destination, from queues that may form at congested routers, or from other sources.

- *Jitter*: Jitter refers to the variability with which packets arrive. For example, the sending host may introduce packets into the network with nice, even spacing. Packets passing through the network that do not encounter congestion will journey smoothly, while those encountering congestion will take longer to arrive. The result is that when the packets arrive at their destination, they will exhibit considerably more variability in spacing than when they were introduced into the network (figure 2-3) (Tanenbaum 2003).

Variations in Different Applications' Need for QoS: Interestingly, applications vary widely in their need for different types of QoS. For example, early Internet applications, such as e-mail and Web browsing, tended to be very tolerant of jitter. Indeed, because both were in essence file-transfer applications, their performance depended entirely on when the last packet of a transmission arrived. So long as the average arrival time was sufficiently short, variability in the arrival times of intermediate packets had no impact on application performance. On the other hand, e-mail and Web browsing place a premium on *reliability* (table 2-2).

For new multimedia applications, such as voice and video, the exact opposite is true: Video-based applications are very sensitive to jitter, as any variability in packet arrival times can cause playback to temporarily lock up and degrade the quality of the end users' experience to unacceptable levels. On the other hand, video does not generally require high levels of reliability. Should any packets turn out to be corrupted or missing, the application can simply process the image without the missing information and proceed to the next image.

FIGURE 2-3
AN ILLUSTRATION OF JITTER

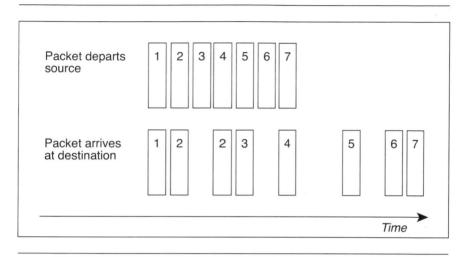

SOURCE: Tanenbaum 2003.

Within all applications, there is a marked difference between pre-recorded and interactive media. For static, prerecorded media, such as songs or movies, a delay of a few seconds is tolerable so long as packets arrive with a steady spacing once the stream begins. In contrast, interactive applications, such as videoconferencing and graphics-oriented gaming, cannot withstand such delays.

Tradeoffs Between Different Types of QoS: Even more importantly, solutions that improve QoS along one dimension often do so at the expense of other dimensions. Consider, for example, the tradeoff between jitter and delay. The classic solution to jitter is to place any packets that arrive in a buffer for a few seconds and then begin to release them at a constant rate. So long as a sufficient quantity of packets is stored in the buffer before playback begins, buffers can smooth out any variability in packet arrival times. The problem is that buffering solves the problems associated with jitter but at the cost of introducing a degree of delay. While effective for prerecorded media, such as movies, this approach

TABLE 2-2

VARIATIONS IN APPLICATIONS' NEEDS FOR DIFFERENT TYPES OF QoS

Application	Bandwidth	Reliability	Delay	Jitter
e-mail	low	high	low	low
bulk file transfer	medium	high	low	low
streaming audio	medium	low	low	high
streaming video	high	low	low	high
VoIP*	low	low	high	high
interactive video	high	low	high	high

* Voice-over-Internet Protocol
SOURCE: Tanenbaum 2003.

will not solve jitter problems associated with interactive media, such as videoconferencing.

Another example is the way TCP prioritizes reliability over delay. As noted earlier, TCP ensures reliability by having the sending host resend any packets for which it does not receive an acknowledgment. In essence, TCP embodies a presumption that the next available window of bandwidth is better used for resending an old packet than for sending a new packet. While valid for file-transfer programs like e-mail and Web browsing, this presumption makes less sense for many forms of video, where if a packet is not ready the moment it is needed, it makes little sense to waste the resources to resend it. Rather than lock up the application waiting for the packet to be resent, video applications would prefer that the sender use the next available window of bandwidth to forward a new packet instead of an old one. Indeed, the existence of applications like voice and video that prioritize delay over reliability is what led the Internet Protocol's (IP's) architects to design the User Datagram Protocol (UDP), which is the other major transport protocol used on the Internet.

Some applications, like bulk-file transfers, demand large amounts of bandwidth and reliability but are very tolerant of delay and jitter. Other applications like VoIP do not require much bandwidth and are tolerant of unreliability but extremely sensitive to delay and jitter. Still others like streaming video require significant amounts of bandwidth and are sensitive to jitter but are tolerant of unreliability and delay. The most demanding interactive video applications, such as video conferencing and virtual worlds, require significant amounts of bandwidth and are intolerant of delay and jitter but can tolerate unreliability.

Both end users and service providers thus face important tradeoffs in deciding how to balance these different aspects of QoS. The fact that applications vary in the types of quality of service that they demand means that the optimal solution for any network provider will depend on the precise nature of the services that its subscribers are demanding from its network.

The Shift from Person-to-Person to Mass Communications

In addition to not being particularly bandwidth intensive, the applications that dominated the network during the ARPANET days (specifically, e-mail and file transfers) consisted almost exclusively of communications from one individual to another. Although the early Internet did contain some point-to-multipoint applications, such as Usenet newsgroups, the vast majority of the traffic was person-to-person. As a result, the Internet was designed around unicast protocols, in which each communication consisted of a single stream of data between two distinct points.

The emergence of the World Wide Web began the Internet's transformation from a platform devoted primarily to person-to-person communications into one for mass communications. This transformation did not stop with the Web: all of the traditional mass media, including newspapers, audio, and video, are in the process of shifting to digital transmission based on the Internet Protocol.

This metamorphosis is effecting a fundamental change in the nature of the network. When communications are person-to-person, individuals are well positioned to ensure that they communicate only with whom they desire. Although the prevalence of telemarketing and spam demonstrate that end users do not have total control over the communications they receive, it is generally up to end users to judge for themselves which communications to accept and which to reject.

The Internet's shift toward mass communications reduces the likely efficacy of relying on individual self-regulation: not every end user can be expected to sift through the avalanche of content that appears on the Internet every day. The result is that end users depend on a wide variety of content aggregators, such as e-mail bulletins, bloggers, and search engines, to help them identify and retrieve previously unseen but interesting content.

Equally important, unicast technologies that set up individual connections for every communication can create serious network-management problems. Consider the 1999 Victoria's Secret fashion show broadcast during Super Bowl XXXIII, which was at the time the most-watched video broadcast in the history of the Internet. The simultaneous attempts by over two million people to connect to the same location overwhelmed the network. As a result, only 2 percent of viewers attempting to access the show were able to do so successfully. In addition, the bandwidth intensiveness of the video broadcast slowed the network to the point where it took more than two and a half minutes to download the Web page. Although networks can avoid this problem by prerecording and caching multiple copies of video programs in locations across the Internet, so-called "flash crowds" continue to be a problem.

Moreover, using traditional unicast protocols to distribute video programming can be extremely inefficient. Unicast distribution meant that Victoria's Secret had to open up thousands of individual communications sessions and send thousands of copies of the exact same packets to the router located closest to its server. A far more efficient solution would have been for Victoria's Secret to send a single copy of its broadcast to its first-hop router and to allow that router and all other downstream routers to duplicate those packets as necessary.

It is for this reason that technologists have been experimenting with *multicasting*, a technology that uses special routers located in the core of the network to keep track of the members of the audience interested in a particular program and the best path to route the data to each of them. These routers then receive a single stream of data from an upstream source and duplicate the stream as many times as necessary to serve all of the interested viewers for which they are responsible.

Note that the need for multicasting necessarily involves placing greater intelligence in the core of the network to duplicate the packets as necessary and to keep track of a forwarding group that is constantly changing as end users join and leave the multicast group. The multicast routers must also incorporate security features to prevent unauthorized sources from misusing the multicast architecture for improper purposes. But upgrading routers to make sure they can support multicasting can be quite expensive.

In addition, multicasting that takes place across multiple networks creates difficult coordination problems: All participating networks must have multicast-compatible routers and must reprogram any network address translators and firewalls that they have deployed in their networks to allow multicast traffic to pass through. They must also find ways to allocate responsibility and to compensate each other for their costs. It is for these reasons that applications that multicast traffic across multiple networks have yet to be widely deployed commercially. Nonetheless, the growing emphasis on IPTV means that the pressure to change the architecture to support multicasting is likely to continue to grow.

The Emergence of Peer-to-Peer Applications

Another major change in the applications running over the Internet is their growing reliance on peer-to-peer technologies. Traditional Internet applications employ what is known as a *client-server architecture*, in which large computers at centralized locations (servers) store files that are then requested by end users (clients). The relationship is generally regarded as hierarchical.

Peer-to-peer technologies follow a very different approach: edge computers in a peer-to-peer architecture are not divided into those that host files and those that request files; instead, computers simultaneously perform both functions. Because this relationship is regarded as less hierarchical than client-server relationships, the computers in this architecture are known as *peers*, and communications between them are known as *peer-to-peer*. Peer-to-peer is thus not synonymous with file sharing or user-generated content, as is often mistakenly assumed. On the contrary, many peer-to-peer applications (such as Vuze) support commercial broadcast services, while many platforms for user-generated content (such as YouTube) employ centralized servers. The real significance of the term *peer-to-peer* lies in the nature of the network architecture.

Whether a network is comprised primarily of clients and servers or of peers has major architectural implications: If a network is organized around a client-server architecture, end users only upload small amounts of code (typically requests for files, such as a uniform resource locator, or URL), and the files they download tend to be much larger. When network owners deployed the basic broadband technologies in the late 1990s, the Internet was dominated by applications—such as Web browsing and e-mail—that adhered to a client-server architecture. As a result, most early broadband technologies (such as DSL and cable modem service) assigned bandwidth asymmetrically, devoting a greater proportion of the available bandwidth to downloading rather than uploading. Although newer versions of DSL and cable modem technology are capable of supporting symmetric service, most continue to allocate bandwidth asymmetrically. Newer broadband technologies, such as wireless video and Verizon's Fiber Optic Service (FiOS), also continue to allocate bandwidth asymmetrically.

These decisions were quite rational when they were made. A network engineer in the mid- to late 1990s, when cable modem and DSL systems first began to be widely deployed, would have had to have been prescient to foresee the eventual emergence of peer-to-peer technologies. The fact that at the time broadband networks were first deployed, network designers did not anticipate end users would serve as well as request files means that these networks may experience significant congestion even if a small number of end users employ their connections to run peer-to-peer applications. As I shall later discuss in greater detail, in last-mile technologies that are most susceptible to local congestion (such as cable modem service and wireless broadband), a relatively small number of end users using peer-to-peer applications can occupy all of the available bandwidth.

The fact that end users are becoming increasingly important sources of upload as well as download traffic is placing great pressure on the limited upload capacity. Recent developments have raised serious questions as to whether a symmetric or an asymmetric architecture will prove to be the better choice in the long run. For the four years preceding 2007, peer-to-peer traffic surpassed client-server traffic in terms of percentage of total bandwidth. A remarkable change occurred in 2007: Client-server traffic began to reassert itself, owing primarily to the expansion of streaming video services, such as YouTube. Some estimate that YouTube traffic constitutes as much as 10 percent of all Internet traffic (Ellacoya Networks 2007). The ongoing transition of high-definition television is likely to cause that demand to increase further still (Swanson 2007). Other video-based technologies—such as Internet distribution of movies (currently being deployed by Netflix), graphics-intensive online games (such as World of Warcraft), virtual worlds (such as Second Life), and IPTV (currently being deployed by AT&T)—are emerging as well (Swanson and Gilder 2008).

The impact has reversed the shift toward peer-to-peer. Ellacoya estimates that between 2005 and 2007, peer-to-peer dropped from 65.5 percent to 36 percent of total traffic and has once again fallen behind Web-based traffic as the leading component of the Internet (2007). Cisco estimates that between 2005 and 2007, peer-to-peer traffic dropped from 68 percent to 51 percent of all consumer Internet traffic and projects that peer-to-peer will drop to 12 percent of all consumer Internet traffic by 2015 (figure 2-4).

FIGURE 2-4
PEER-TO-PEER AS A PERCENTAGE OF CONSUMER INTERNET TRAFFIC

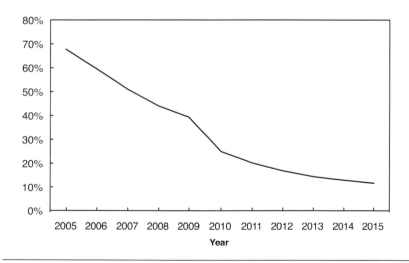

Year

SOURCES: Cisco Systems (2007, 2008b, 2009, 2010b, 2011b).

Measured in terms of the ratio of upload traffic to download traffic, the pattern of traffic associated with peer-to-peer applications differs starkly from that associated with applications based on client-server architectures. Traditional Internet applications generate traffic primarily when the end user is actually seated at the keyboard submitting network requests. Personal computers (PCs) running peer-to-peer applications can place requests for files and respond to requests for files twenty-four hours a day even when the end user is not at the keyboard, thereby causing them to generate traffic constantly. In addition, because peer-to-peer technologies involve machine-to-machine communications, they often introduce traffic into the network in a more sustained and intensive manner than client-server technologies. The result is that the lion's share of upload traffic is generated by a small number of super-heavy peer-to-peer users. As few as 5 percent of end users may be responsible for generating more than 50 percent of all Internet traffic (Vorhaus 2007; Levy 2008).

The design of some peer-to-peer applications, such as BitTorrent, has an even more distinct effect on the network: Instead of serving files from a location, BitTorrent divides files into multiple pieces and stores duplicate copies of each piece in multiple locations. When a BitTorrent user attempts to retrieve a file, the software avoids the congestion that can result from downloading the entire file from a single location by initiating parallel sessions with multiple peers, each of which serves only part of the file. This by itself represents a fairly substantial deviation from the pattern of network traffic associated with client-server architectures. Moreover, BitTorrent has the ability to identify those connections with the highest transmission speeds and the greatest available capacity and to redirect traffic onto those links. The effect is to saturate the bandwidth of whichever network has spent the most to expand its capacity.

Cloud Computing

Cloud computing represents one of the hottest topics in information technology today. Under the traditional paradigm, the software and data run by end users are stored locally on the host computer's hard disk. Under cloud computing, both the software and the data reside in a facility known as a *data center* and are accessed on demand. The only software needed on the end user's device is a *thin client*, such as a browser, capable of providing access to the application residing in the data center.

Proponents of cloud computing predict that it will yield substantial benefits. Cloud computing can allow multiple customers to share the same hardware within the same data center, thereby allowing smaller companies to take advantage of scale economies that they could not realize on their own. Even companies that are large enough to achieve minimum efficient scale by themselves may see advantages. The fact that hardware represents lumpy, indivisible investments that must typically be provisioned in advance means that companies risk running out of capacity should demand grow more rapidly than anticipated. Conversely, they may face the burden of fallow resources should demand grow unexpectedly slowly. The fact that companies must provision hardware for peak demand also means that cloud computing is particularly helpful when demand is highly variable, since aggregating demand lowers variability. The greater dispersion made possible by virtualization can reduce latency and increase reliability (Weinman 2011). Cloud computing also greatly simplifies the applications running on end users' machines, which reduces the cost of end-user devices. Centralization reduces the cost of rolling out upgrades.

Predictions about the future of cloud computing run the gamut, with some forecasting that all information technology will eventually migrate into the cloud (Carr 2008) and with others criticizing it as nothing more than overhyped repackaging of existing technologies (Ellison 2009). What is even less well understood is what increasing use of cloud computing would mean for the network architecture.

End-User Connectivity: Cloud-computing customers need different services from their last-mile networks. Since the software and data needed to run applications no longer reside on end users' hard disks, cloud computing needs more ubiquitous connectivity and more substantial uptime guarantees than have previously been necessary. Because data processing no longer occurs locally, reliance on cloud computing also increases demand for the quantity of bandwidth as well as its ubiquity.

Moreover, because cloud computing provides services that used to be delivered by corporate intranets, cloud-computing users may well demand higher levels of quality of service from their last-mile networks. These demands will likely vary from company to company. For example, financial-services companies typically require perfect transactions, with latency guarantees measured in microseconds. In addition, the provider must be able to verify the delivery time of each and every transaction after the fact. The fact that information that used to reside exclusively within an end user's hard disk and processor must now be transmitted over the network also means that cloud-computing customers are likely to demand higher levels of security from their last-mile networks as well as more control over the paths that key traffic takes than the current decentralized routing architecture permits.

Data Center Connectivity: The advent of cloud computing also requires improvements in data center connectivity. As an initial matter, customers establishing new cloud-computing instances must provision their data to the data center. Because datasets in the terabyte range would take weeks to upload, many cloud-computing providers recommend that customers download their data onto a physical storage medium and send it via an overnight mail service, such as FedEx (Brodkin 2010).

The agility and virtualization demanded by cloud computing also require the flexibility to move large amounts of data between data centers very quickly. The best-efforts architecture of the current Internet cannot offer the guaranteed levels of quality of service that these functions require. For this reason, many cloud-computing providers interconnect their data centers through dedicated private lines. Others have begun outsourcing these services to other networks, partially to gain the economies of sharing resources with others and partially out of concern that they will be classified as common carriers. On a more radical level, some industry observers predict that cloud computing may require assigning separate addresses to each individual machine and to the location where the application that the machine is accessing resides (Nemertes Research 2007).

Privacy and Security: Finally, cloud computing has fairly significant implications for privacy and security. As an initial matter, cloud computing often requires large amounts of data that previously did not leave a corporate campus to be shifted from one data center to another. In addition, virtualization necessarily envisions that these data will reside on the same servers as other companies' data. As a result, the hardware located in these data centers and the networks interconnecting them require a higher level of security than previously necessary. Industry participants are also often very protective of information about the volume and pattern of their transactions. They are thus likely to impose stringent requirements on what data can be collected about their operations and how those data are used.

The fact that data may be shifted from one data center to another also potentially makes those data subject to another jurisdiction's privacy laws. Because customers are ultimately responsible for any such violations, they are likely to insist on a significant degree of control over where the data reside at any particular moment.

The Emergence of the App Store and the Changing Nature of the Essential Platform

The emergence of smartphones represents a fundamental shift in the dominant platform for Internet-based communications. Throughout most of its history, the vast majority of Internet traffic consisted of content delivered through a browser. Although different content providers could use Java scripts to add different types of functionality, Java and the browser remained the dominant Internet platform. The advent of the iPhone has marked a fundamental shift away from this architecture. Instead of running on a browser, iPhone apps typically run directly on the smartphone's mobile operating system.

The shift in focus away from content running on a browser and toward an application running on an operating system has important implications. As an initial matter, the entire purpose of an iPhone application is to provide access to specifically targeted content and to make this content more prominent and more easily accessible than other content. Modern smartphone applications (apps) are thus not general-purpose platforms providing equal access to different types of content. On the contrary, by their very nature, smartphone apps are designed to discriminate content.

Additionally, the essential platform has changed. Instead of access to the browser interface, the key platforms are the mobile operating system and the application store. At this time, there is a vibrant competition among different mobile operating systems, with each one tied to a different company's smartphone. As a result, device manufacturers now play a more central role in the value chain than was previously the case.

Lastly, the emergence of smartphone apps represents a fundamental change in the business model underlying the Internet: Unlike traditional Internet content, which end users have come to expect to be free from access charges and supported exclusively by advertising, smartphone apps must be purchased by individual consumers before they can be used.

* * *

The ways in which the nature of the applications running on the Internet has changed since the Internet first emerged in the mid-1990s is placing tremendous pressure on the network to evolve in response. If the Internet is to allow consumers to realize the potential benefits implicit in these new technologies, it will have to develop the architectural means to support all of these new uses. Unfortunately, the current policy debate remains rooted in the vision of the Internet when it first emerged as a mass-market phenomenon in the mid-1990s. The emergence of applications that are increasingly bandwidth intensive and more demanding in terms of QoS, that are composed of mass communications rather than person-to-person communications, employ alternative approaches such as peer-to-peer distribution and cloud computing, and that are comprised of individual applications running directly on an operating system rather than different forms of Java-enhanced content running through a browser are all placing increasing pressure on the network to develop in new directions to meet end users' changing demands.

3

The Diversification of
Transmission Technologies
and End-User Devices

Internet technologies have undergone significant changes since the mid-1990s. When the Internet first emerged, end users were linked to it almost exclusively through connections provided by the local telephone company. In addition, end users almost universally connected to the Internet through the same device: a desktop personal computer.

This chapter explores how increased diversity in the technological environment over the past decade has changed the industry. End users now connect to the Internet through an ever-broadening array of last-mile networking technologies and devices. As we shall see, this poses new challenges.

The Growing Diversity of Transmission Technologies

One of the biggest changes in the Internet since the mid-1990s is the increase in the number and variety of last-mile networking technologies. As noted earlier, when the Internet first emerged, end users connecting from home employed dial-up modems to make calls through the local telephone network to offices maintained by Internet service providers. End users connecting at work or from school connected to the Internet via a T-1 line or some other high-speed technology also provided by the local telephone company.

As of the late 1990s, Internet users began to migrate from narrowband to broadband services. In the process, they began to connect through a much broader range of transmission technologies, whose characteristics vary widely in terms of available bandwidth, reliability, susceptibility to local congestion, and problems associated with addressing and routing. These differences in technical challenges and opportunities have naturally led engineers to move away from simplistic one-size-fits-all solutions and instead rely on responses tailored to each particular technical situation.

Cable Modem Systems: The early leader in the broadband race was cable modem service, which offers high-speed Internet service via channels on the coaxial cables that have traditionally been used to provide multichannel cable-television services. Cable modem systems originally employed a standard known as data over cable service interface specification (DOCSIS) 1.0, which used one television channel to support a maximum theoretical download speeds of 27 million bits (or 27 megabits) per second (Mbps), with actual download speeds running closer to 6 Mbps. In 2008, cable modem providers began wide-scale deployment of DOCSIS 3.0, which currently bonds four television channels to support a theoretical maximum of 160 Mbps and to deliver actual download speeds of around 50 Mbps. DOCSIS 3.0 permits cable operators to increase capacity further by bonding additional channels.

Digital Subscriber Lines: Cable modem providers soon faced competition from a telephone-based broadband technology known as *digital subscriber line* (DSL) service. DSL takes advantage of the fact that conventional voice communications only occupy the lower transmission frequencies without affecting higher frequencies. DSL uses those higher frequencies on the existing copper telephone lines to transmit data communications without interfering with voice communications. The primary variant of DSL, known as *asymmetric DSL* (ADSL), supports download speeds of up to 3 Mbps and upload speeds of 768,000 bits (or 768 kilobits) per second (kbps). AT&T and Qwest are currently deploying an even faster version known as *VDSL*, or *very high bit rate digital subscriber line*, which is capable of providing theoretical download speeds of up to 100 Mbps. As of March 2011, AT&T's U-verse network offered download speeds of up to 24 Mbps to 28 million homes, with an ultimate target of 30 million homes by the end of 2011. In July 2010, Qwest began rolling out its VDSL-based Heavy Duty Internet service, which offered speeds of up to 40 Mbps to 4.5 million homes as of the end of 2010.

Fiber-to-the-Home: The highest bandwidth transmission technology is *fiber-to-the-home* (FTTH). The U.S. industry leader is Verizon's fiber-based FiOS network, which provides download speeds of up to 50 Mbps to 16 million homes (roughly half of its service area) and is ultimately expected to reach 18 million homes. Tests indicate that FiOS is capable of supporting speeds of up to 10 billion bits (or 10 gigabits) per second (Gbps).

Wireless Broadband: But perhaps the most dramatic development in recent years has been the rapid growth of wireless broadband technologies. Mobile-phone providers have increasingly offered data services on third-generation wireless platforms that typically achieve download speeds of up to 1.4 Mbps. Competition is also beginning to emerge from unlicensed wireless technologies such as Worldwide Interoperability for Microwave Access (WiMax), with Clearwire projecting to deliver download speeds of 3 to 6 Mbps to 119 million people in over 70 cities by the end of 2010.

Fourth-generation wireless services, such as *Long Term Evolution* (LTE), are projected to offer download speeds up to 12 Mbps, with a theoretical maximum download speed of 173 Mbps. Verizon began wide-scale deployment of LTE in December 2010. As of May 2011 its LTE network covered 110 million people with plans to cover 185 million by the end of 2011.

The meteoric rise of mobile wireless broadband services is captured by the broadband data collected by the Federal Communications Commission (FCC) (figure 3-1), although the analysis is complicated slightly by a change in methodology that caused a one-time drop in the number of wireless broadband subscribers in December 2008. Though the FCC has begun to collect data on higher tiers of service, historical information is available only for one category: high-speed lines, defined as services that provide at least two hundred kbps in at least one direction. Measured in terms of high-speed lines, mobile wireless broadband went from having essentially no subscribers as of the end of 2004 to having over 84 million subscribers and just under 46 percent of the market by December 2010.

FIGURE 3-1

U.S. SUBSCRIBERS TO HIGH-SPEED LINES BY TECHNOLOGY (MILLIONS)

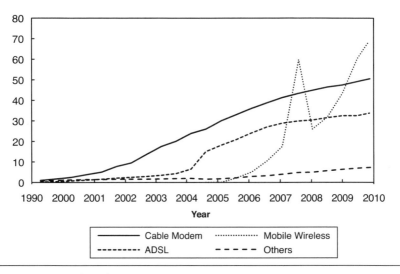

SOURCES: FCC 2007 and 2011b.

Wireless broadband is becoming increasingly ubiquitous. The most recent data published by the FCC indicate that as of July 2010, 98.5 percent of the U.S. population is served by at least one mobile-broadband provider. At the same time, wireless broadband is becoming more competitive, with 91.9 percent of the population served by at least two wireless broadband providers and 81.7 percent of the population being served by at least three (table 3-1).

The data suggest that wireless broadband has the potential to become a game changer in terms of broadband policy. Even taking into account the sharp drop in the number of wireless broadband subscriptions at the end of 2008 caused by the FCC's change in methodology, it is clear that wireless has emerged as a ubiquitous and competitive platform for broadband services that is likely to become even more significant in the years to come.

TABLE 3-1

NUMBER OF WIRELESS PROVIDERS BY CENSUS BLOCK, 2010

Number of Providers	Population (millions)	% of Total U.S Population
1 or more	281.0	98.5
2 or more	262.1	91.9
3 or more	233.0	81.7
4 or more	193.4	67.8

SOURCE: FCC 2011a.

Broadband Technologies' Technical Differences

Although the market for last-mile broadband services has become much more competitive over the past decade, it would be a mistake to assume that each of these technologies is fungible and that all of them can be managed in exactly the same manner. On the contrary, important technical differences exist that cause the challenges that each technology faces to vary widely.

Bandwidth Limitations and Capital Costs: The policy debate is just beginning to recognize the significant variations in the way that these different technologies operate and how those variations affect public policy. These differences mean that each will require distinctly different network-management techniques.

Perhaps the most striking difference among these various technologies is the amount of bandwidth available to each. As noted earlier, FTTH has the most bandwidth, with a capacity that is expandable into the gigabit range. Next come cable modem systems, with a maximum theoretical speed of 160 Mbps and expandable by shifting more video channels to broadband service, followed by VDSL, which tops out at 100 Mbps. The lowest speeds are currently offered by wireless broadband, although the impending deployment of fourth-generation services should reduce that gap considerably. Unlike other technologies, which can simply build larger pipes, the limited amount of spectrum available strictly constrains wireless broadband providers' ability to expand capacity.

Congestion Management: The various broadband technologies also vary widely in their susceptibility to local congestion, which is not a major problem for telephone-based technologies (such as DSL and FiOS), where traffic is not shared with others until it is aggregated at the central office or at a remote terminal. Because the level of aggregation tends to be in the tens of thousands of subscribers, variations in particular individuals' usage patterns tend to cancel one another out, which insulates end users from the impact of what their immediate neighbors are doing.

The reality is quite different for cable modem providers. End users in a cable modem system share bandwidth with the roughly five hundred other households sharing the same neighborhood node. This means that they are very sensitive to what their immediate neighbors are doing. As few as ten to fifteen people using BitTorrent can cause everyone's service sharing that node to slow to a crawl (Martin and Westall 2007).

Wireless broadband is similarly subject to local congestion problems. Unlike telephone-based technologies, which give each subscriber a dedicated connection, wireless broadband providers connect to the Internet through transponders located on microwave towers that must be shared with other customers in the same area.

In other words, cable modem and wireless broadband are subject to local congestion problems to which telephone-based technologies are immune. This problem is exacerbated in the case of wireless broadband by another consideration: In DSL and cable modem systems, broadband traffic is carried in a channel that is separate from the channels delivering those providers' other services. Thus, broadband traffic cannot degrade the quality of service of telephone and cable companies' core business offerings, no matter how much that traffic increases. This is not true in the case of wireless, which shares bandwidth with the voice services offered by wireless companies. Consequently, any congestion that may arise in a wireless broadband network degrades not only the quality of Internet broadband services provided but also the conventional voice services that represent the wireless providers' core business.

The fact that wireless devices tend to move frequently from one cell to another also means that they tend to drop packets with a much higher frequency than do wireline technologies. This in turn requires wireless technologies to manage congestion in a different manner from wireline technologies.

The seminal moment in the history of congestion management occurred in the ARPANET (a government-funded precursor to the modern Internet) during the mid-1980s, where a series of *congestion collapses* caused the network to slow to a crawl. The problem was an unexpected consequence of the way reliability is ensured by TCP (Transmission Control Protocol, the primary protocol used on the Internet). As noted in the previous chapter, TCP expects receiving hosts to send acknowledgments for every data packet that they receive. Sending hosts that do not receive an acknowledgment within the expected time frame resend the packet, after which point two duplicate packets are flying through the network, doubling the number of packets carried by an already over-burdened network. The failure to receive an acknowledgment for those packets caused the host to introduce still more packets into the network. This eventually caused the network to enter a state similar to gridlock. Like gridlock, the congested state can become stable and persist long after the problem that initially caused the congestion has dissipated.

Congestion arises when multiple hosts attempt to use the network at the same time. Managing congestion thus depends on knowing how a wide range of hosts is using the network at any particular time. Individual hosts, however, typically lack any information about what other hosts are doing. Unless some mechanism is devised for providing them with information about the level of congestion in the network, hosts are generally poorly situated to take the lead role in managing congestion. The logical solution as a theoretical matter would be to give the routers operating in the core of the network primary responsibility for managing congestion. Unfortunately, routers are extremely expensive to upgrade and reconfigure, and the fact that the Internet is comprised of multiple autonomous systems means that there has been no one in a position to push through a global change to the routing architecture.

Van Jacobson (1988) devised an ingenious solution to this problem when he identified a way for hosts operating at the edge of the network to infer when the network is congested. Jacobson recognized that networks typically drop packets either because (1) a transmission error caused a packet to become corrupted or (2) congestion caused a buffer in one of the routers to become full, which in turn forced it to discard a packet. Because wireline networks are sufficiently reliable, in that they rarely drop packets because of transmission errors, Jacobson realized that hosts operating at the edge of the network could take a missing acknowledgment as a strong signal that the network is congested. He therefore devised a protocol that requires hosts that fail to receive an acknowledgment to alleviate congestion by cutting their transmission rates in half.

This solution quickly became the primary mechanism for managing congestion on the Internet. Indeed, it remains so today. It is, however, subject to a number of technical limitations. As discussed in the previous chapter, because it depends on acknowledgments, this management system does not work for protocols that do not use acknowledgments, such as UDP. Although this was not a problem when TCP represented the vast majority of network traffic, the advent of VoIP and IP video has made UDP an increasingly important component of network traffic. Projections indicate that UDP will continue to represent a larger proportion of network traffic for the foreseeable future.

In addition to the difficulties in managing traffic associated with IP video, Jacobson's algorithm is poorly suited to managing congestion in wireless networks. Recall that his approach is based on the inference that a dropped packet is the result of congestion and not transmission error. While this inference is sound for the high-reliability environment of wireline networks, it is poorly suited to the high-loss environment of wireless networks, where, as noted above, packets are often dropped for reasons other than congestion. Consequently, the assumption that a missing acknowledgment is a sign of network congestion (which represents the foundation for the basic approach to managing congestion on the Internet) does not apply to wireless technologies.

Even worse, packet loss due to congestion and packet loss due to transmission errors call for diametrically opposed responses. When the network is congested, hosts must reduce their transmission rates exponentially. Continuing to send at the same rate risks inducing congestion collapse. By contrast, when a packet is lost because of transmission error, reducing the sending rate is the worst possible reaction. On the contrary, the optimal action would be for the host to resend the dropped packet as quickly as possible without slowing down its sending rate at all. Any slowdown in the transmission rate will simply degrade the efficiency with which the network is being utilized. Taking an approach to congestion management that was developed for wireline networks and applying it to wireless networks thus causes the network to respond in precisely the wrong way.

And so wireless network congestion is managed quite differently from wireline network congestion. One possible solution to this muddle is for sending hosts to be aware of when they are communicating with a wireless host and to take steps to distinguish between losses caused by transmission error and those losses caused by congestion. Other solutions place responsibility for resending lost packets on the routers operating in the middle of the network rather than on the hosts operating at the edge of the network, by storing copies of packets bound for mobile hosts, monitoring the return traffic for missing acknowledgments, and resending any packets that are lost due to transmission failure. Still other solutions call for split connections, in which the sending host establishes one TCP connection with an IP gateway located in the middle of the network and employs a separate TCP connection between the IP gateway and the receiving host. Many of these solutions violate the semantics of IP. All of them require introducing traffic-management functions into the core of the network to a greater extent than originally envisioned by the Internet's designers (Tanenbaum 2003; Kurose and Ross 2010).

Together, these technical differences in susceptibility to local congestion and to transmission errors make it sensible for different transmission technologies to manage congestion in different ways. Simply put, cable modem and wireless broadband providers will take steps to manage local congestion that telephone companies do not need to take. Moreover, running the same congestion-management protocols across all transmission technologies will cause TCP-based applications to run more poorly on wireless networks than on wireline networks. The lower reliability of wireless networks also requires that they employ a completely different means for managing congestion than do wireline networks. Although such deviations from the status quo may have the effect of treating some traffic differently, they do not necessarily harm consumers or innovation. Instead, they may be better regarded as the natural response to the growing heterogeneity of transmission technologies.

The Physics of Wave Propagation: Wireless technologies are subject to a wide range of technical limitations and challenges not faced by wireline technologies. For example, the performance of wireless broadband networks is affected by environmental factors (such as topography, foliage, buildings, and moisture) to a much greater extent than that of wireline technologies.

The physics of wave propagation create numerous complexities for wireless networks with which wireline technologies need not contend. As an initial matter, wireless transmissions attenuate more quickly with distance than do wireline transmissions. Furthermore, wireline signals are channeled by the physical medium in a single direction. The extreme directional focus of wireline transmission means that adjacent signals tend not to interfere with one another, even if they are extremely close together. Wireless signals, by contrast, typically propagate outward in all directions and are perceived as background noise by adjacent wireless users. Claude Shannon (1948a and 1948b) showed long ago that the maximum transmission rate of information along a bandwidth-limited channel is largely a function of the signal-to-noise ratio, with increases in the noise floor lowering the total throughput rate. This implies that increases in the number of wireless users degrade the usable bandwidth of other users transmitting in the same vicinity. It also implies that there is an absolute limit to the number of wireless users that can operate in the same geographic area, a limitation that does not exist for wireline technologies. After a certain point, the addition of any additional wireless signals would render communication completely impossible (Gupta and Kumar 2000). Although receivers can compensate for this problem if they know the direction from which the interference is occurring, they cannot do so when the locations of the transmitters are constantly changing, as with mobile wireless devices.

Wireless transmissions are also susceptible to "multipath" problems, in which an end user's own signal becomes a source of interference for its own transmission. Much as yelling across a canyon can create echoes, wireless signals can bounce off terrain or other physical features in ways that cause the same signal to be reflected back toward the person generating it. These reflections can cause the same signal to arrive at the receiver multiple times: once on a direct line from the transmitter and again later as an echo. In short, the same signal can reach the same destination along multiple paths.

Depending on the details of the physical environment in which a transmitter is operating, multipathing can cause a wireless transmitter to interfere with its own signal. And the problem is exacerbated by the fact that sound is composed of sine waves: If multiple waves of the exact same shape arrive exactly in phase with one another, they can reinforce each other. If they arrive exactly out of phase, they tend to cancel each other out. The former effect is illustrated by the phenomenon of "whispering corners," in which someone whispering in one corner of a room can be heard clearly in the opposite corner even though he or she is facing the opposite direction and located many feet away. The latter effect is illustrated by the sound-dampening system employed by Bose headphones and many cars, which retransmit sounds to eliminate ambient noise.

Because multipathing represents interference from a signal with the exact same shape as the original signal, it can reinforce or dampen wireless transmissions exactly in this manner. It can thus create hot and cold spots that are located extremely close together. Moreover, multipathing depends on the precise configuration of hard objects off which the wireless transmissions can reflect. This includes not only stationary objects, such as buildings and terrain, but also mobile objects, such as cars and buses.

In May 2010, at a conference held at the University of Pennsylvania, one participant related a particularly vivid example of this phenomenon: While living in London, he deployed a directional antenna to provide Wireless Fidelity (WiFi) service to the famous Speakers' Corner in Hyde Park, only to find his signal intermittently negated despite the absence of any direct obstructions. He eventually discovered that the interference arose whenever a double-decker bus was forced to stop at a nearby traffic light. Even though the bus did not directly obstruct the signal traveling between his flat and the Speakers' Corner, it created a multipath reflection that canceled out the direct signal (Sandvig 2010).

The end result is that wireless transmissions are much more subject to interference from the environment and other users than are wireline transmissions. Moreover, this interference results from both stationary and transient features, rendering the performance of wireless networks unpredictable and dynamic from moment to moment. Thus wireless providers incorporate different architectural principles into their networks to reflect these important technological differences.

Wireless Networks and the Lack of IP Addresses: One of the central architectural principles underlying the Internet is that every end node must be able to connect to every other end node. The Internet's current design achieves this by assigning every host a unique IP address visible to all other hosts on the network. This organization assumes that IP addresses change relatively infrequently, allowing TCP and UDP sessions in essence to take the existing address architecture as given for the entirety of their sessions.

But the mobility made possible by wireless networking is exerting extreme pressure on this system of network management. The traditional model implicitly assumes that end users connect to the Internet via a desktop PC. Because PCs do not frequently change locations, a single address could identify both the device as well as the location at which that device is connected. The emergence of wireless broadband has caused the unity of identity and location implicit in IP addressing to break down. Unlike PCs, mobile devices, such as laptops and smartphones, may connect to the network in any one of a wide number of physical locations.

It is for this reason that some engineers have proposed modifying the address space in a way that would assign separate addresses for devices and locations. Other engineers believe that such solutions are too radical and unnecessary for wireline technologies.

Instead of implementing the more radical solution of creating an identity-locator split, it is also theoretically possible to modify the existing IP protocols to keep the network updated regarding all address changes in the network. The current standard for IP mobility solves this problem by having each wireless host designate a router on its network as a *home agent* that will serve as the initial contact point for all IP-based communications addressed to that host. Each remote network similarly establishes a *foreign agent* to serve as the central contact point for all communications terminating on that network. Users who wish to contact the mobile user initiate contact with the home agent, which then forwards the packets it receives to the mobile device's current location.

The process is surprisingly complex. The mobile IP protocol must perform three primary functions. The first is agent discovery, in which mobile hosts' home agents and foreign agents willing to serve mobile hosts communicate their willingness to play these roles to the rest of the Internet. The second is allowing the mobile host and the foreign agent to which it is currently connected to notify the home agent of its current location. The third is determining the manner in which the home agent will forward packets to the remote agent. To complicate the matter further, each of these three functions is sufficiently nuanced.

Moreover, this solution to IP mobility suffers from *triangle routing*, an inefficiency that occurs because traffic sent from one location to another must necessarily traverse a third location before reaching its final destination. Suppose, for example, a person who usually resides on the East Coast is traveling to the West Coast. If the person sitting next to him attempts to send him a message, it will have to travel all the way across the country to that person's home agent and then back again in order to reach its destination, even though the sending and receiving hosts are only located a few feet apart.

Current wireless broadband systems avoid these difficulties by forgoing Internet-based protocols to connect to mobile hosts. Instead, the universal practice now is to rely on legacy telephone-based technologies to maintain and update wireless connections. Stated in technical terms, wireless networks currently manage mobility at Layer 2 of the Internet protocol stack instead of Layer 3, where the IP addresses reside. As a result, all current wireless broadband devices lack the end-to-end visibility to interact with the Internet on the same terms as fixed PC-based connections.

Fourth-generation wireless technologies, such as LTE, are expected to rectify this shortcoming soon. Until that occurs, wireless devices will necessarily connect to the Internet on different terms and in a less interoperable manner than devices transmitting through traditional wireline connections. And once the shift to LTE takes place, providers will have to resolve how to best manage the increased complexity of addressing in wireless networks.

The engineering community has not yet determined which approach will ultimately prove optimal. Until a consensus emerges, network providers are likely to deploy a wide range of solutions, some of which may not be fully interoperable, and some of which may do a better job transmitting certain types of traffic than others. Policymakers should be careful not to foreclose experiments with different approaches until those managing portions of the network are able to make a clearer determination about which technological approach to pursue.

The Economics of the Next Generation of Bandwidth Expansion

The current wave of broadband technologies also differs from the first wave in terms of the capital costs needed to deploy them. The first round of upgrades to broadband technologies was based on cable modem systems and DSL. Because these technologies leveraged legacy investments in existing communications networks, they could be implemented relatively cost effectively, typically costing somewhere in the neighborhood of $400 to $800 per subscriber. The relatively small size of these capital investments meant that they could easily be recovered with only a modest increase in the monthly revenue generated from each customer.

The broadband technologies that are providing the basis for the current wave of bandwidth expansion are quite different. Consider Verizon's FiOS network: Unlike technologies that leveraged legacy technologies, FiOS requires laying down an entirely new distribution grid in addition to fairly significantly reconfiguring the way the network terminates at the end users' premises. FiOS carries a total price tag of $23 billion, and financial analysts estimate the cost of the FiOS buildout at roughly $4,000 to $5,000 per customer. Even the most optimistic estimates put forward by Verizon imply a total cost of at least $2,400 per customer. Fourth-generation wireless technologies face costs that are likely to be steeper than DSL and cable modem service, with the spectrum costs alone in the 700 MHz auction running $19.6 billion, with AT&T committing to invest another $19 billion to improve its current mobile broadband network. Estimates place the cost to provide 100 Mbps in bandwidth to 100 million homes at a minimum of $350 billion, which again implies a cost recovery in the thousands of dollars.

Although the National Broadband Plan includes a recommendation of $30 billion to help extend the network, those funds have yet to be appropriated. And even if that level of support were to emerge, it would have to be followed by appropriations of roughly ten times the size in order to finance upgrading network capacity. The fact that the current political debate is focusing on ways to reduce rather than increase government spending makes such expenditures unlikely for the foreseeable future. In the absence of government funding, covering these higher costs will necessarily require a much more substantial increase in revenue than was needed during the previous rounds of bandwidth expansion. The industry should expect these providers to offer new types of premium services and to search for new ways to monetize potential revenue streams. The success of this and future rounds of bandwidth expansion depend on it.

The Growing Diversity of End-User Devices

Another major technological change in recent years concerns the devices that end users employ to connect to the network. When Internet usage was first popularized during the mid-1990s, almost all users connected through desktop PCs. By their nature, PCs have generous amounts of memory, storage capacity, and computing power. Because they draw electricity directly from the wall, PC-based connections did not need to economize on power consumption. The robustness of PC-based computing platforms meant they were not particularly sensitive to conflicts between applications.

Today, however, end users employ a much broader array of devices to obtain Internet service. Perhaps most striking in this development is the proliferation of advanced mobile wireless devices that contain computing power beginning to rival that of early PCs. The advent of smartphones is placing an enormous amount of pressure on network capacity, since their additional functionality is causing the intensity of network utilization to increase sharply. For example, given AT&T's initial exclusivity arrangement with the iPhone, one might have expected that the iPhone's success would in turn benefit AT&T. What happened instead is that iPhone users downloaded applications and content at two to four times the rate of other smartphone users, the most popular iPhone applications tending to be particularly bandwidth intensive. All of this strained AT&T's network enormously.

Furthermore, compared to PCs, mobile devices are much more limited in terms of memory, storage, and computing power, and they are extremely sensitive to conflicts between applications and to power consumption. Smartphones are competing vigorously in terms of input interfaces (including touch screens and reduced-size keyboards) and have yet to settle on a single operating system. The result is that the functionality provided by different wireless devices varies widely. Moreover, some wireless networks attempt to minimize the impact of bandwidth scarcity by prioritizing time-sensitive applications, such as voice, over applications like e-mail, which can better tolerate a delay of a few seconds. This type of network management typically requires tight integration between the network and the device. As a result, industry observers have concluded that the device has become an inextricable part of the functionality of the network (Jackson 2011).

The universe of devices should become even more heterogeneous in the future. Presently, there exists a vast array of options offering more limited functionality. Netbooks, for example, are low-cost computers that focus on providing wireless connectivity and a limited number of applications like e-mail and Web browsing, offering more sophisticated applications via Web-based service providers. And other devices are even more specialized. Electronic readers, such as the Amazon Kindle, only support reading eBooks. Other specialized devices, such as gaming consoles and portable media players like the Apple iPod, incorporate network connectivity, but only for limited functions. Still other devices offer greater functionality while not matching that of a stationary PC. A leading example is the tablet PC, which includes handwriting recognition functions that allow end users to input data using a stylus or a finger instead of a keyboard and a mouse.

Pervasive Computing and Sensor Networks: Another innovation in the devices attached to the edge of the network is the result of the emergence of sensor networks and pervasive computing. Manufacturers of cars, home appliances, and other consumer devices are increasingly incorporating computer chips into their products. Furthermore, *radio frequency identification* (RFID) chips are being attached to an increasing number of objects. The wireless signal from a sensor can provide enough power to activate RFID chips even though they do not possess their own power source. Familiar uses of RFID chips include the prevention of shoplifting, inventory management, and automated collection of tolls on highways.

The scholarship on pervasive computing and sensor networks has primarily focused on privacy concerns. In the process, the literature has largely overlooked the extent to which these technologies require different services from the network. For example, pervasive computing and RFID chips require ubiquitous networking that provides reliable last-mile connectivity in a much broader range of locations than traditional Internet applications. These technologies also have the potential to increase dramatically the number of devices that will require network visibility, which will place further pressure on an Internet Protocol version 4 (IPv4) address space that is rapidly nearing exhaustion. The fact that the locations of these end points typically change rapidly may require some fundamental changes to routing and addressing systems.

In addition, the technology underlying these devices is quite different from the typical desktop PC in ways that may require some network-architectural modifications. As an initial matter, RFID tags and other pervasive computing devices may lack the power and functionality to send acknowledgments in response to every packet received. As a result, the network architecture may have to take a fundamentally different approach to ensuring reliability and managing congestion than it does with respect to other technologies. Moreover, the specialized nature of many of these devices may require a much tighter integration with the network than is typically required of PCs.

Because RFID tags and pervasive computing devices may perform only limited functions, they may not require individual IP addresses. If so, they would probably reside behind an IP gateway and use a Layer 2 protocol to make the final connection. Such a development would prevent these devices from being fully visible to other actors on the Internet and would place functionality in the core of the network in ways that would contradict the principle favoring end-to-end visibility to all edge-connected devices.

* * *

In sum, the past decade has seen a fairly dramatic increase in the heterogeneity of the technologies comprising the Internet. The growing technological diversity of the network underscores the benefits to crafting solutions tailored to particular technological environments and counsels strongly against continued reliance on one-size-fits-all solutions.

4

The Upsurge in the Complexity of Business Relationships

Although commentators and policymakers pay lip service to the fact that the Internet is a "network of networks," their analyses all too often speak of the Internet as if it were a single, unified entity instead of a collection of 35 thousand autonomous systems bargaining with one another through arms-length transactions. Therefore, anyone involved in broadband policy must understand how those autonomous systems relate to one another, both in terms of the physical configuration (known as the network's topology) and in the economic terms under which they interconnect.

Just as the universe of end users, applications, and technologies has grown larger and more heterogeneous over the past fifteen years, so have the business relationships underlying the Internet. In any system comprised of 35 thousand independent actors, wide variations in the terms under which various components interconnect are inevitable. Indeed, such variations typically represent either the type of experimentation associated with a healthy, innovative environment or a natural attempt to respond to economic conditions that vary across the network and over time.

That said, certain patterns exist in the way that the business relationships are changing; these patterns are sufficiently widespread and systematic such that they yield insights into the changing of network operation. Understanding these patterns can also guide policymakers as they evaluate the likely impact of various regulatory proposals.

FIGURE 4-1
THE NSFNET BACKBONE, CIRCA 1992

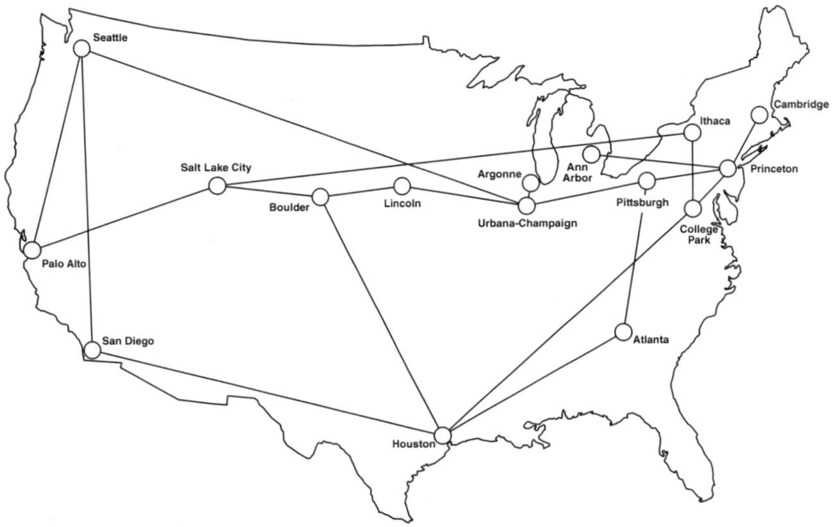

SOURCE: Merit Network 1996.

The Topology of the Early Internet

Before discussing how the topology of the network is changing, one must first have a clear grasp of the way the network was configured before these changes started to occur.[5] When the Internet was first developed, its topology and the business relationships comprising it were relatively simple. As is widely known, the Internet evolved out of the National Science Foundation Network (NSFNET) backbone, which was created in 1986 to provide universities all over the country access to a small number of federally funded supercomputing centers (figure 4-1).

The NSFNET's architects gave the Internet a tripartite structure (figure 4-2): At the top was the NSFNET backbone, which interconnected a small number of supercomputing centers and other research facilities. At the bottom were the campus networks run by individual universities that

---

[5] For a more extended analysis of the discussion that follows, see Yoo 2010c.

FIGURE 4-2

THE NSFNET THREE-TIERED NETWORK ARCHITECTURE

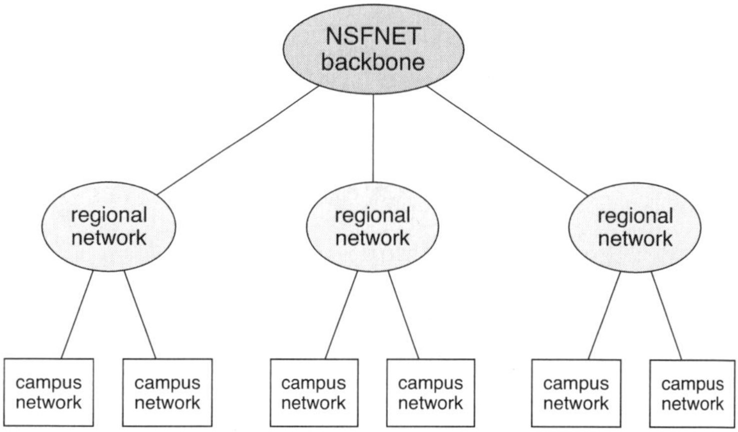

SOURCE: Merit Network 1996.

provided the final connections to end users. The gap located between the campus network and the nearest supercomputing center was filled by regional networks (typically operated by university consortia or state-university partnerships) that provided connectivity from distant locations and the NSFNET backbone's interconnection points.

The resulting topology organized the network into a series of parallel hierarchies, all of which interconnected at the top layer in the NSFNET backbone. Every packet traveling through the network had to traverse what were essentially identical paths that passed up and down through each level of this three-level hierarchy. For example, a campus network would take the traffic it was originating and hand it off to the regional network with which it was associated. The regional network would then hand the traffic off to the NSFNET backbone. The backbone would then route the traffic to the appropriate regional network. That regional network would in turn pass the packets on to the campus network that was the ultimate destination. The routing architecture of the day only permitted each campus network to connect to a single regional network.

FIGURE 4-3

THE HIERARCHICAL STRUCTURE OF THE INTERNET
AFTER BACKBONE PRIVATIZATION

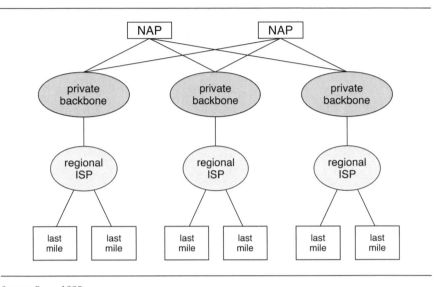

SOURCE: Braun 1995.

The network largely retained this same basic architecture when it was privatized during the mid-1990s. The campus networks at the bottom of the hierarchy were replaced by last-mile providers that transport traffic from end users' residences and places of business to local distribution facilities maintained in individual cities. In the case of telephone-based technologies, these providers are usually called *central offices*, whereas they are typically termed *headends* in the case of cable modem systems. The regional networks evolved into regional ISPs that transport traffic between the central offices and headends maintained by last-mile providers to the backbone interconnection points. The NSFNET backbone at the top of the hierarchy was replaced by a series of private backbone providers (figure 4-3). Because the backbone now consisted of multiple providers instead of a single network, the NSF had to devise a way for backbone providers to exchange traffic with one another. To facilitate these transfers, the NSF established four public peering points, also

FIGURE 4-4

THE NETWORK HIERARCHY DEPICTED AS A SERIES OF CONCENTRIC RINGS

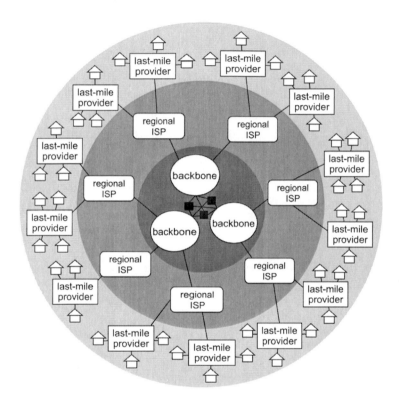

SOURCE: Author's illustration.

sometimes called *network access points* (NAPs), located in San Francisco, Chicago, New York, and Washington, D.C.

The privatization of the Internet did not change the hierarchical nature of the basic architecture. Each regional ISP still connected to a single backbone, and each last-mile provider still connected to a single regional ISP. Indeed, the early versions of the protocol employed by the backbones to route traffic would not support more complex topologies. Because backbones can properly be regarded as representing the core of the network, this hierarchy is often depicted as a series of concentric circles, with backbones sitting in the innermost ring, regional ISPs residing in the middle ring, and last-mile providers sitting in the outermost ring (figure 4-4).

The use of one-to-one relationships conferred a number of advantages: This architecture constituted a "spanning tree" that connected all of the nodes with the minimum number of links. Furthermore, because only one path existed between any two nodes, the network did not need to make any complex determinations regarding the path along which particular traffic should be routed (Spulber and Yoo 2005).

That said, tree architectures suffer from a number of drawbacks. Hierarchical structures make each network participant completely dependent on the players operating at the level above, which in turn provides backbones with a potential source of market power (Besen et al. 2001). The uniqueness of the path connecting any two nodes means that the failure of any link or node in the network will inevitably disconnect part of the network. Moreover, even when all network elements are operating properly, any congestion that arises at any network element will cause the quality of service provided to every downstream element to deteriorate. Indeed, the NAPs became particularly congested, with estimates of packet loss at times running as high as 40 percent (*Red Herring* 1999).

This problem has become particularly acute in the modern Internet, in which extremely popular events can create flash crowds that in turn can cause large portions of the network to fail, such as occurred during the Victoria's Secret broadcast in 1999, as described in chapter 2.

Private Peering Points

Over time, networks began to experiment with different network topologies to deal with these problems. These innovations include private peering points, multihoming, secondary peering, content delivery networks, and server farms (figure 4-5).

As noted earlier, one of the first problems to emerge in the early Internet was congestion in the public NAPs, which often degraded throughput times and network reliability. Congestion has led companies to establish additional NAPs in such locations as Los Angeles, Dallas, and San Jose to alleviate the congestion in the original NAPs established by the NSF.

FIGURE 4.5

PRIVATE PEERING

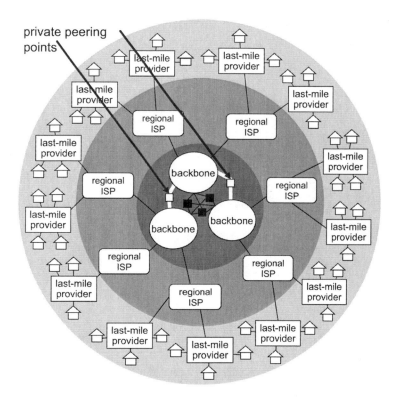

SOURCE: Author's illustration.

In addition, backbones entered into private interconnection agreements that bypassed the NAPs altogether and instead exchanged traffic at private interconnection points. Not only did the bilateral nature of the exchange make it easier for them to avoid congestion and preserve quality of service (Faratin et al. 2008); it also gave backbones the freedom to exchange traffic at more cost-effective locations. For example, under the original architecture, traffic traveling between different autonomous systems in Europe would often have to travel across the Atlantic Ocean and back. The establishment of new interconnection points in Europe

FIGURE 4-6
MULTIHOMING

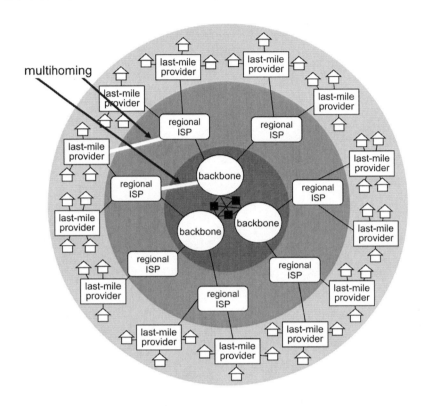

SOURCE: Author's illustration.

obviated the need to incur the additional delay and expense of two unnecessary transoceanic trips (Paltridge 1998; Kende 2000).

Multihoming

As noted earlier, the initial protocol responsible for routing traffic on the Internet implicitly assumed that any pair of end points was connected by a single, unique path. As a result, routing only permitted each last-mile network to connect to a single regional ISP and each regional ISP to connect to a single backbone.

In the late 1990s, the protocol running the backbone (known as *Border Gateway Protocol*, or BGP) was revised to permit more complex interconnection arrangements. The current version, known as BGP4, supports less hierarchical routing structures and no longer requires that the connection between any two locations be unique.

As a result, network providers began to establish connections with multiple actors located in the higher levels of the hierarchy. Last-mile providers began to establish relationships with multiple regional ISPs. Regional ISPs also began to establish relationships with multiple backbone providers (figure 4-6).

Multihoming provides end users with a number of benefits: As an initial matter, the existence of multiple paths through which traffic can reach a particular end user greatly increases the network's reliability. This is of critical importance to many end users, as evidenced by the fact that corporations typically connect with multiple telecommunications providers so that backup possibilities are always available.

Multihoming also mitigates whatever market power is possessed by upstream network providers (such as backbones). The presence of alternative paths to connect to the Internet naturally limits every market participant's ability to raise price (Besen et al. 2001; Economides 2008).

The presence of multiple connections to the Internet also allows end users to manage congestion. If all of the traffic sent by an end user had to travel through a single connection, periods of heavy usage would cause that connection to become quite congested. The presence of multiple connections allows the end user to use a *load balancer* to distribute packets among all of those connections so that no one connection has to bear the weight of all of the traffic.

Allowing end users to redistribute traffic dynamically across these connections can also reduce cost. Much as mobile-telephone consumers pay a flat fee for a predetermined number of minutes and then pay on a per-minute basis for any overages, enterprise users typically prepay for a fixed amount of bandwidth (known as the *committed rate*) and pay a volume-related charge. An end user with multiple connections would want to exhaust his committed rate on each connection before incurring any overage charges and even when exceeding the committed rate would want to minimize peak usage by dividing traffic across all of his connections.

The most sophisticated load balancers can also enhance quality of service by pinging both lines and then routing the most time-sensitive traffic along the fastest connection. This approach prioritizes certain traffic, while forcing other traffic to travel over a slower connection. Enabling such traffic management can enhance the benefits that the end user derives from the network.

Secondary Peering

In the early Internet, network providers interconnected through two types of contracts. Backbones (also known as tier 1 ISPs) entered into *peering* relationships with one another, in which they exchanged traffic on a settlement-free basis and no money changed hands. Transaction costs offer the primary justification for forgoing payment. Although the backbones could meter and bill each other for the traffic they exchanged, they could avoid the cost of doing so without suffering any economic harm so long as the traffic they exchanged was roughly symmetrical.

But severe traffic imbalance would render such arrangements uneconomical. Thus tier 1 ISPs will not peer with other networks that are unable to maintain a minimum level of traffic volume. In addition, peering partners typically require that inbound and outbound traffic be roughly balanced by requiring that each partner's traffic not fall outside a 2:1 or 1.5:1 ratio. Regional ISPs and other networks that cannot meet these requirements must enter into *transit* arrangements, under which they pay the backbone to provide connectivity to the rest of the Internet.

Regional ISPs that did not have sufficient volume to peer with tier 1 backbones found that they did have sufficient volume to peer with each other. In so doing, they established a practice termed *secondary peering*, which created a collar of interconnections surrounding the backbones (Yoo 2006; Kende 2000; Faratin et al. 2008) (figure 4-7).

The creation of alternatives to backbone services has made the Internet less hierarchical. Indeed, as much as 70 percent of the nodes in the Internet can now interconnect with one another without passing through

FIGURE 4-7

SECONDARY PEERING

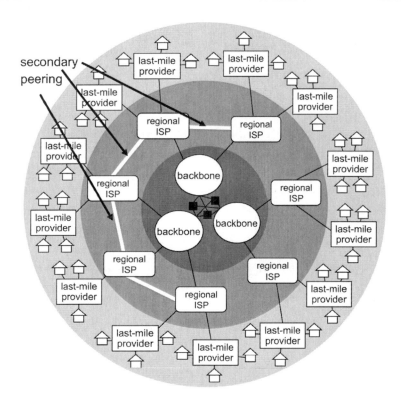

SOURCE: Author's illustration.

the public backbone (Carmi et al. 2007). The weakening of the centrality of the backbones' position has the salutary effect of reducing their market power and limiting their ability to obtain a competitive advantage by cutting off access to part of the network or by degrading service. The addition of multiple connections also helps manage complexity by helping to keep the average path length manageable. The shortcuts associated with secondary peering and multihoming prevent the average path length from increasing logarithmically with the scale of the network, as predicted by the theoretical models (Zhao et al. 2008).

Secondary peering creates other advantages for end users as well. As was the case with multihoming, increasing the number of paths for traffic enhances the network's reliability and robustness. In addition, secondary peering reduces the size of the transit charges that regional ISPs must pay to backbones, which in turn reduces the cost of network service borne by end users. In many cases, secondary peering would improve network performance by shortening the number of hops needed to reach certain destinations.

Deviating from the traditional hierarchy necessarily means that not all traffic will pass equally through the network. Suppose, for example, that the regional ISP serving a particular end user has a secondary peering relationship with the regional ISP serving one news website (such as CNN.com) but not another news website (such as MSNBC.com). The result is that content from CNN.com will probably arrive more quickly than content arriving from MSNBC.com. Because traffic arriving from CNN.com will not have to pay transit charges to the backbone, it will unquestionably arrive more cheaply. The result is that these two similarly situated content providers will receive different levels of service and face different costs. The cause is entirely the result of each website's location in a decreasingly hierarchical network topology.

Content Delivery Networks

CDNs represent another emerging innovation in the Internet's topology (figure 4-8). Akamai, the market leader, serves more than 15 percent of the world's Web traffic. Instead of delivering content from a central location, Akamai caches Web content at over sixty-five thousand servers located in one thousand ISPs in seventy countries around the globe.

Substituting storage for long-distance networking resources in this manner yields several benefits. Caching content closer to end users reduces latency and transmission costs. In addition, storing content at multiple locations instead of at a single location allows the CDN to redirect requests dynamically. In so doing, the CDN can ensure that content is delivered even if flash crowds or denial-of-service attacks congest particular servers. CDNs may yield economic benefits as well.

FIGURE 4-8
CONTENT DELIVERY NETWORKS

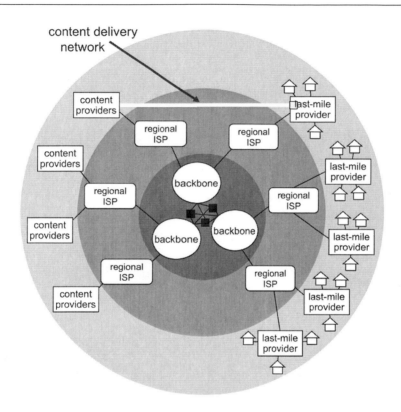

SOURCE: Author's illustration.

By connecting directly to last-mile providers, CDNs simplify bargaining by reducing the number of parties that must be involved in negotiating end-to-end service. Negotiating interconnection agreements directly with last-mile providers also makes it possible for network actors to move money back and forth across a peering point (Clark et al. 2006).

Because CDN content is typically served locally, it represents a fairly significant deviation from the hierarchical topology that has traditionally dominated the Internet. To the extent that Akamai links its caches via private connections, it can bypass the public backbone altogether. CDNs thus represent an innovative way to deal with the increasing complexity of the Internet. CDNs work best for static content; they are less well suited to delivering interactive content that changes dynamically. In addition, CDNs are commercial services. The greater reliability and quality of service are thus available only to those who are willing to pay for them.

Server Farms

In addition to using overlay networks like CDNs and employing network providers that are experimenting with different topologies, large content providers are taking things into their own hands, building *server farms*, large facilities that store and distribute content locally without having to traverse the public backbone, in much the same manner as CDNs. Indeed, a recent study indicates that Google, Yahoo!, and Microsoft have been able to use server farms to bypass the backbone altogether for roughly a third of their traffic and to keep their number of hops for traffic that had to pass through the backbone to no more than one or two (Gill et al. 2008).[6]

Server farms yield much the same benefits as CDNs. Positioning content closer to end users reduces latency and transit costs. The serving of content from a network of distribution sites protects content against server congestion and denial-of-service attacks. Increased reliance on private networks also gives the content providers greater control over network security and performance. It is also possible that server farms give large content providers a de facto entry barrier that protects them against smaller content providers. Server farms may well simplify bargaining, reduce costs, and allow increasingly varied pricing relationships to the point where they become essential to competing effectively. The problem is that small content and application providers may lack sufficient scale to support large data centers of their own.

---

[6] For press accounts documenting the proliferation of server farms, see Raynovich 2005; Markoff and Hansell 2006; Mehta 2006; and Vance 2009.

Implications

All of these developments represent innovative solutions to the changing realities of the Internet. The differences in network topology mean that traffic that is otherwise similar may travel through the network at different speeds, with different costs, and with greater security and protection against congestion. The actual performance will depend on the specific relationships that the network provider has negotiated with other providers as well as the end user's willingness to pay.

These deviations from the strict hierarchy that characterized the early Internet are simply the reflection of network providers' experiments with new ways to reduce costs and ensure quality of service. They do make simple generalizations about network neutrality and equality of treatment quite problematic.

Part II

POLICY IMPLICATIONS

5

Changes in the Optimal Level of Standardization

How should the network respond to such dramatic changes in the end users, applications, technologies, and business relationships comprising the Internet? The chapters in this second part explore possible responses, beginning in this chapter with the effect of these changes on network standardization.

Standardization is often touted as one of the Internet's most generative features. Ensuring that the entire network operates on a single, uniform set of principles allows end users to access content all over the world regardless of its location. In addition, standardization is said to spur innovation by guaranteeing those developing Internet-based content and applications access to the entire universe of potential customers (Carpenter 1996; Lessig 2006).

Despite these benefits, not all goods in every market are standardized, and consumers often benefit from being able to purchase more customized offerings. The question is how to determine when particular products should be standardized and by how much.

Fortunately, the study of economics gives us some simple tools for analyzing the impact that the changes discussed in part I will have on the optimal level of standardization. Simply put, as the technological and economic environment diversifies, society would be best off if the services provided by the network were to diversify as well.[7]

---

[7] For a more extended discussion, see Yoo 2005.

The Impact of Increasing Heterogeneity of Consumer Preferences

Consider first the impact of the increasing diversification of the universe of Internet end users and applications. The economic literature suggests that the optimal level of standardization is largely a function of the heterogeneity of demand. If everyone wants the same thing from the network, the optimal outcome is to provide a single network designed to deliver exactly what people want. However, if what people want from the network varies, end users would, then, be better served were network providers to offer *different* types of services designed to meet the needs of the smaller subgroups of the larger market.

Stated somewhat more formally, the burgeoning literature on network economic effects offers some simple but powerful insights into the benefits of standardization.[8] Network economic effects exist when the value of the network increases with the number of other users connected to the same network. The classic example is the telephone, whose value to the end user increases as the number of people reachable through that telephone network increases. So too, growth in the number of people subscribing to the network thus increases its value even if the physical handset, the quality of service, and the cost of service remain unchanged.

Consider the classic standards competition between the VHS and Beta formats for videocassette recorders (VCRs), a scenario recently replayed in the battle between the Blu-ray and HD DVD formats for high-definition video discs. In both cases, would-be purchasers of consoles did not focus much on the technical characteristics or even the price of each platform, where both platforms appeared to be more than adequate. The most important consumer consideration ended up being the platform other people would adopt. In the case of VCRs and video disks, end users did not benefit directly from the ability to physically connect to other end users through the network. Instead, they benefited indirectly from the wide availability of movie titles in their chosen format. In other words, network economic effects can create benefits directly from being able to reach more people through the network or indirectly through the greater availability of complementary goods.

---

[8] The seminal article on network economic effects is Rohlfs 1974. For a survey of the literature, see Farrell and Klemperer 2007.

The literature on network economic effects is quite controversial, with some commentators arguing that it frequently leads to market failure and others contending that it does not.[9] For our purposes, it suffices to note the implications of this literature for standardization. There are real benefits derived from standardizing on a particular network format. The literature on network economic effects has long recognized, however, that these benefits require some qualifications. For example, in most cases the benefits of belonging to a larger network are subject to diminishing marginal returns. In other words, the increase in value caused by adding an additional subscriber is probably more when doing so increases the size of the network from one hundred to one hundred and one than when the additional subscriber increases the network from one million to one million and one. In addition, the growing heterogeneity of end users means that they will value the ability to connect to some endpoints much more highly than others. To use a personal example, my own network usage disproportionately consists of connections to only a handful of sites: my own e-mail server, remote access to the desktop in my office, the Penn Law School's website, and a handful of news, weather, and financial-services sites. When end users' demands focus on a small number of sites, they may well place a higher value on better connections to those sites than on being able to access a greater number of sites.

Most importantly, standardization inevitably causes a reduction in product variety (Farrell and Saloner 1985 and 1992; Katz and Shapiro 1994; Liebowitz and Margolis 1996). No standard can be optimized for every contingency. As a result, every standard inevitably performs certain functions better than others. In choosing to standardize on a single format, end users must inevitably forgo the potential benefits that other formats could provide. In short, by its nature standardization necessarily causes a reduction in product variety.

This sacrifice should not be particularly great if consumer preferences are uniform, because the fact that all end users want the same thing from the network enables the network architect to satisfy all of their preferences with a single design. It becomes more difficult to satisfy end users with

---

[9] For leading articles identifying ways in which network economic effects can lead to market failure, see Farrell and Saloner 1985 and Katz and Shapiro 1985. For contrary points of view, see Liebowitz and Margolis 1996 and Yoo 2002.

a single standard as their network needs and wants become increasingly diverse. Eventually, consumer preferences become so heterogeneous that it becomes optimal for network providers to offer multiple standards. In the extreme case, providers will offer completely separate networks, as is the case with companies establishing private networks with dedicated connections. In less extreme cases, providers will offer networks that interconnect with one another, but in ways that will support certain applications and end users better than others.

These dynamics are captured nicely by a simple model developed by Farrell and Saloner (1986b). Their model shows that end users will standardize on a single network only if the benefits they derive from being part of a larger network exceed the costs of adopting a standard less well fitted to their particular needs. If end-user preferences are sufficiently different that they would derive substantial benefits from adopting an incompatible standard, end users will do so. The question is which of these two effects dominates. Most interestingly, Farrell and Saloner's model indicates that end users choose incompatibility only when it is socially beneficial. End users may choose to standardize, however, even when society would be better off if they chose incompatibility.

This suggests that excessive incompatibility is not as significant a problem as the danger of too much standardization. And this finding is consistent with the literature suggesting that end users may either be too reluctant or too eager to change standards (Farrell and Saloner 1986a; Katz and Shapiro 1992) as well as the extensive literature warning how network economic effects can cause a network to become "locked in" to an obsolete standard (David 1985; Farrell and Saloner 1985; Arthur 1989; Katz and Shapiro 1994). Any remaining concerns about having multiple, incompatible networks can be ameliorated if a bridge technology exists that allows the two networks to interconnect with one another, even if that interconnection is imperfect.[10]

This literature suggests that the natural response to the increasing diversity in what end users want from the network is a lower level of

---

[10] If the adapter technology serves as a perfect bridge between the networks, incompatibility creates no social harm whatsoever (Katz and Shapiro 1985). If the adapter is imperfect, the presence of the bridge technology may or may not maximize social welfare, depending on the circumstances (Farrell and Saloner 1992).

network standardization. As discussed in chapter 2, end users' demands on the network are becoming more heterogeneous. Those using interactive video services like video conferencing and role-playing games are demanding lower latency. Those deploying health care–monitoring applications are demanding greater reliability. Those migrating to cloud-computing applications are demanding greater connectivity assurances, throughput rates, and security. And many different users are demanding additional bandwidth. Put a slightly different way, the increasingly specialized services being offered by network providers may be nothing more than their natural attempt to satisfy consumer demands that are increasingly varied. Imposing regulation to stop these kinds of innovations would harm rather than help consumers.

The following example may help illustrate my point. Consider a network comprised of three players of roughly equal size who all interconnect via the same standard. Suppose further that one of those players wanted to deviate from the standard. Should regulatory authorities allow it to do so?

Three possible outcomes exist. First, the deviator may have found a new business model that provides benefits to all end users, in which case stopping it from adopting this new strategy would be the worst thing possible for consumers. Instead, this player should be permitted to go forward, stealing customers from its competitors until they make the same change. Second, the deviation may turn out to be a terrible idea, in which case the firm deviating from the existing standard will lose customers until it once again returns to the fold. Third, the deviation may be better for some consumers but not for others. If that is the case, the firm deviating from the existing standard may be able to pursue a niche strategy by targeting a smaller subgroup within the larger market that places a particularly high value on a specific type of service. Adopting a niche strategy can allow network providers to survive despite being relatively small and facing diseconomies of scale, much in the way boutiques continue to survive in a world increasingly dominated by low-cost discounters. In fact, differentiation could permit three different types of networks to coexist: one optimized for traditional conventional Internet applications such as e-mail and website access, another incorporating security features designed to appeal to users focused on e-commerce, and a third offering prioritized service needed to support delay-sensitive applications. If such differentiation were to occur, the upside associated with offering more customized services can offset the downside of belonging to a smaller network.

This example illustrates how permitting network participants to deviate from the existing standard can promote greater competition in the last mile by enabling the survival of firms operating at a cost disadvantage. Standardization also tends to commodify network services, which forces firms to compete solely on price and network size, which in turn reinforces the advantages enjoyed by the largest players. Conversely, increasing the dimensions along which networks compete not only benefits consumers directly by giving them a broader range of choices but also benefits them indirectly by making it easier for multiple last-mile providers to coexist.

The Impact of Increasing Heterogeneity in Technology

In addition to requiring homogeneity in demand, standardization of the network on a single protocol also requires that all network providers face the same cost structure. If the costs faced by different network providers are widely divergent, one would expect the providers to adopt very different solutions. The increasing technological heterogeneity discussed in chapter 3 thus represents an additional impetus toward nonstandardization that complements the effect of the increasing heterogeneity among Internet users and applications. Given the growing divergence of technologies, the differences in *cost* would lead one naturally to expect different portions of the network to balance the relevant tradeoffs in different ways.

Consider the differences in network capacity, which remains one of the most significant differences among the various transmission technologies. The question is how to design a network to ensure that latency-sensitive traffic does not encounter delays. One way to ensure that video and other delay-sensitive traffic passes through the network without disruption is to overprovision the network—that is, to build excess capacity so that there is sufficient headroom to accommodate any short-term bursts of activity that may occur. Unfortunately, deploying excess capacity is expensive and effectively raises the revenue and the number of customers needed for a service to break even. As a result, relying on overprovisioning as a means to guarantee QoS will limit build-out, particularly in those rural and urban areas most adversely affected by the digital divide. Networks can avoid having to include excess bandwidth if they can instead manage traffic when demand surges, protecting the end-user experience by giving a higher priority to traffic that is sensitive to delay.

A comparison between Verizon's fiber-based FiOS strategy and AT&T's VDSL-based U-verse strategy illustrates the point nicely: The greater bandwidth available to FiOS gives it the capacity to offer multichannel video without having to engage in any traffic management. The more limited bandwidth available to U-verse requires that it employ a wide variety of network-management techniques in order to provide the guaranteed throughput rates needed to provide multichannel video in an acceptable manner. For example, unlike FiOS and cable television systems, which broadcast all of the channels that they offer regardless of whether the subscriber is viewing those channels or not, U-verse conserves bandwidth by employing a *switched digital video* technology that only transmits the channel the subscriber is actually watching. In addition, U-verse also ensures the quality of its video service by prioritizing its video over other traffic. If it were not to do so, U-verse would be unable to complete the triple play by offering multichannel video in addition to voice and data without incurring the multibillion-dollar expense of building a fiber network of its own.

The difference between the FiOS and U-verse strategies exemplifies one of the classic tradeoffs in network management. Internet traffic is notoriously volatile, with sudden bursts occasionally causing network demand to surge (Leland et al. 1994). When traffic peaks in this manner, it often causes periods of congestion that can be difficult to anticipate. When this occurs, the resulting congestion causes network traffic to slow down. While a delay of a half-second is essentially inconsequential to first-generation Internet applications (such as e-mail and Web browsing), such delays can render newer applications (such as IP video and VoIP) unusable. Theoretical models suggest that such traffic-management techniques can reduce the amount of bandwidth needed by more than 60 percent (Houle et al. 2007). Comparing FiOS and U-verse, consider FiOS's cost of $23 billion and U-verse's more modest price tag of $7 billion.

Wireless broadband networks also employ similar network-management techniques. When a wireless broadband subscriber is at a low-bandwidth location, wireless broadband providers prioritize voice and other delay-sensitive traffic over packets associated with applications that are more delay tolerant, such as e-mail. Some wireless broadband providers take the even more extreme step of banning video, peer-to-peer, and other bandwidth-intensive applications altogether; this is demonstrated eloquently by placards aboard the Amtrak Acela express trains asking passengers to refrain from using the WiFi service to download video and is demonstrated further by the decision by those providing wireless broadband over unlicensed spectrum to prohibit end users from running peer-to-peer applications or downloading video. Aggressive usage by a single user can effectively render the service unusable for everyone else.

Which strategy represents the better strategy has divided the engineering community, with some believing passionately that overprovisioning represents the best course and others believing just as passionately in the merits of network management (Comer 2006; Kurose and Ross 2010). The financial markets are similarly undecided. Wall Street initially reacted quite skeptically to Verizon's FiOS strategy (Kolodny and Szalai 2006). Since that time, Verizon's ability to hit its projected targets has made some critics more sanguine, while others still remain unconvinced and argue it will take more than a decade to determine whether Verizon's investments will pay out in the end (Hansell 2008).

The point at which the engineering and financial communities remain so sharply divided over the best course of action is precisely the point at which policymakers should refrain from intervening by mandating one particular solution over the other. Instead, policymakers should create regulatory structures that give industry participants the freedom to pursue different business strategies until sufficient data develop to determine the circumstances under which one or the other approach would be preferable.

Other technical differences among the various technologies lead providers to adopt very different approaches to managing their networks. As noted in chapter 4, cable modem and wireless broadband systems are much more susceptible to local congestion than are telephone-based broadband services. As a result, we should expect cable modem and wireless broadband providers to manage local congestion much more aggressively than do telephone companies. Although such measures can easily be portrayed as anticompetitive, they can instead be regarded as the natural consequence of differences among these various technologies. Similarly, the fact that wireless broadband networks face much greater variations in reliability forces them to manage their networks far more aggressively than cable- and telephone-based broadband providers.

Thus, the growing heterogeneity of technologies comprising the Internet should inevitably cause differences to emerge among the ways different types of providers manage their networks. It would thus be a mistake to presume that deviations from the current standard are motivated by anticompetitive concerns. On the contrary, the economic literature suggests that the much greater danger is insufficient rather than excessive willingness to deviate from the status quo. Policymakers should thus take care not to impose regulatory regimes that impede the network from following its natural evolutionary path. Instead, they should adopt a regime that allows different types of experiments to go forward, while reserving the right to step in after the fact should any harm to consumers emerge.

6

The Inevitable Decline
of Informal Governance

During its initial years, the Internet was characterized by relatively informal mechanisms of governance. Spam and other antisocial activity were kept in check by teaching new users the proper standards of "netiquette." The entire domain name system was overseen by a single person, with disputes often settled by a simple handshake. The IETF, which as noted earlier is the Internet's primary standard-setting organization, followed a decidedly informal governance process. Membership was open to anyone willing to attend the meetings. Decision making tended to be informal and consensus based, with agreement often signaled through the rather curious institution of humming (Hoffman and Harris 2006).[11]

At the same time, members of the Internet community expressed hostility toward formalized decision making. Speaking for the online body, David Clark (1992), DARPA's chief protocol architect during the 1980s, declared at the 1992 IETF meeting, "We reject: kings, presidents and voting." Or as John Perry Barlow (1996) said even more colorfully, "Governments of the Industrial World, you weary giants of flesh and steel, I come from Cyberspace, the new home of Mind. On behalf of the future, I ask you of the past to leave us alone. You are not welcome among us. You have no sovereignty where we gather." Instead, members of the community embraced self-governance based on principles developed from the bottom up (Johnson and Post 1996).

---

[11] Bradner (1999) describes the advantages of using humming as a polling mechanism: "The difficulty in determining whether or not any particular person is humming makes it a relatively private form of voting. The fact that it is hard to hum louder makes it hard for a minority to use loud voices to exaggerate the level of support for their position."

But the previous decade's growth in the number and diversity of end users has undermined the preconditions for this informal system of governance. Although Internet-related institutions still pay obeisance to the original norms of informal, consensus-based decision making, the governance itself has become more formal. Indeed, the theoretical writings analyzing when informal governance does and does not work suggest that this transformation was inevitable.

The Importance of Close-Knit Communities

The primary way to understand the circumstances under which informal governance works is through the literature on social norms, pioneered by Robert Ellickson (1991) and Nobel laureate Elinor Ostrom (1990), which examines when parties are able to resolve disputes without having to resort to formal governance mechanisms. Social norms theory recognizes that communities, rather than relying on law, often rely on informal sanctions, such as loss of reputation and ostracism, to ensure conformity with societal expectations. In order for these informal means of governance to be effective, however, the community must typically be close knit, in that the people comprising the community must be relatively few in number, be homogeneous in interest and background, and interact with each other in a wide range of overlapping contexts.

Although the Internet might once have been a close-knit community, the rapid growth of the Internet since the mid-1990s makes any such claim about today's online body untenable. As noted in chapter 1, not only has the number of users exploded, but their growing diversity means they hold a wide variety of values and cannot reasonably said to be anchored by a common set of experiences and expectations. The multiplicity of purposes to which they are putting the network has also undermined the previous alignment of goals. In addition, the increase in the number of users has caused them to become increasingly atomized and anonymous.

One natural consequence of these developments is that the informal governance mechanisms that have previously governed the Internet will certainly begin to break down (Lemley 1998; Radin and Wagner 1998;

Hetcher 2001). The following case studies show how this norm-based approach has already begun to be replaced by more formal modes of governance in three contexts: spam control, the domain name system, and congestion management.

Spam Control

Perhaps the most eloquent example of the breakdown of informal governance is the problem of unsolicited e-mail, more commonly known as spam. The watershed moment in the history of spam occurred on April 12, 1994, when Laurence Canter and Martha Siegel, a husband and wife team of immigration lawyers, sent an advertisement to six thousand Usenet groups offering to help interested parties apply for a green-card lottery. Until that time, the Internet community had succeeded in using informal sanctions to keep such commercially oriented communications to a minimum. But this time was different. The so-called "green-card spam" was a financial success, netting the couple $100,000. Despite a firestorm of criticism from other users and the revocation of their subscription by their ISP, Canter and Siegel remained unrepentant, vowing to advertise again and even publishing a book telling others how to send similar ads (Canter and Siegel 1994). Eventually, though, Canter was disbarred in part because of his participation in this advertising campaign.

Since that fateful day, spam has grown to become an all-too-familiar part of the Internet landscape. The *New York Times* reporter who covered Canter and Siegel's story correctly recognized that their green-card spam was a reflection of the increasing diversity of the universe of Internet users: "The incident underscores the growing conflict between newcomers who want to exploit the commercial potential of the internet, and the original Internet community, which arose as a government and academic network and has long shunned the more commercial nature of such popular public services as CompuServe, Prodigy, and America Online" (Lewis 1994). And in an interview eight years later, Canter opined that the change in online behavioral norms was a reflection of the times and that it had been only a matter of time before anyone would have begun sending spam (Feist 2002).

The breakdown of informal governance opened the door to more formal systems of governance. Indeed, problems with spam have prompted even those sympathetic to preserving the Internet's existing architecture to call for new measures that hold spammers more accountable (Minar and Hedlund 1999). Over time, thirty-six states went on to enact laws restricting spam. Finally, in 2003, Congress enacted the Controlling the Assault of Non-Solicited Pornography and Marketing (CAN-SPAM) Act, establishing a national regime for controlling spam that criminalized forging headers, using deceptive subject lines, and omitting return addresses from e-mails and that required senders to remove recipients who object from their distribution lists.

The CAN-SPAM Act's inability to stem the flow of spam that still inundates end users' inboxes every day should not obscure its larger significance. People continue to debate ways to make the legal regime more effective. But at this point, no one is advocating a return to the cooperative, norm-based modes of governance that limited the abuse of spam prior to the mid-1990s. The growth in the size and diversity of the population of Internet users has turned the informal system for curbing spam into a relic of the past.

The Domain Name System

Another classic example of the formalization of Internet governance is the *domain name system* (DNS), which determines which parties are entitled to use certain Web addresses. Between 1977 and 1998, responsibility for decisions about Internet addresses rested with the Internet Assigned Numbers Authority (IANA), which at the time was essentially the alter ego of a single person, Jonathan Postel, who had begun running the domain-name system while a graduate student at UCLA. Postel essentially singlehandedly maintained a comprehensive list of domain names and the IP addresses to which they corresponded in a single file known as *the root*. Domain name disputes were resolved informally, usually sealed with handshake agreements rather than formal contracts.

Two factors eventually undermined this system of informal controls. First, the growth of the number of hosts attached to the network made it impossible for a single person to update the root fast enough to keep up with the Internet's growing scale. Second, the emergence of the Internet as an important forum for commerce made control over domain names (particularly those containing trademarks) more important.

Eventually, through a process overseen by the U.S. government, the overall responsibility for managing the DNS was vested in a new entity known as the Internet Corporation for Assigned Names and Numbers (ICANN). Although ICANN continues to pay lip service to the legacy of informal governance by espousing a commitment to "achieving broad representation of global Internet communities" and "developing policy...through bottom-up consensus-based processes" (ICANN n.d.), its decision-making process is generally regarded as quite formal.

ICANN's decision-making processes have drawn sharp criticism for being cumbersome and undemocratic. But even ICANN's harshest critics recognize that the transition away from informal governance was inevitable once the community of stakeholders grew larger, more dynamic, and more heterogeneous (Liu 1999; Zittrain 1999; Weinberg 2000; Mueller 2002).

Congestion Management

As the emphasis on formal governance mechanisms has grown since the mid-1990s, the network's approach to managing congestion has similarly formalized. As noted in chapters 3 and 4, the Internet relies primarily on a simple, edge-based mechanism to manage congestion. Whenever a host running TCP at the edge of the network fails to receive an acknowledgment, it interprets the missing acknowledgment as a sign that the network is congested and cuts its sending rate in half.

The system's weakness where managing congestion is concerned centers on its dependency on the voluntary cooperation of end users. This is because certain changes to the Internet environment have made such cooperation less likely to occur. For example, recall our chapter 3 discussion of the growing importance of delay-sensitive, bandwidth-intensive applications, such as IP video. As noted earlier, because such applications prioritize minimizing delay over ensuring reliability, they use a protocol known as UDP that forgoes the use of acknowledgments to confirm that each packet has been received intact. Because UDP does not use acknowledgments, the congestion-management system described above will not work for UDP. Instead, the network depends on each host to deploy a system that ensures that its UDP data streams do not consume more bandwidth than the typical TCP data stream (Braden et al. 1998; Floyd and Fall 1999).

Even hosts running acknowledgment-based protocols—like TCP—can pose a significant problem for congestion management. As noted in chapter 4, the current system of congestion management depends on hosts running TCP to cut their sending rate in half whenever the failure to receive an acknowledgment signals that the network is congested. The problem is that the hosts' incentives to comply with this regime are too weak. From the selfish perspective of a particular host, the ideal solution to clear the network of congestion would be to continue to send packets into the network at an accelerated rate while depending on all other hosts to reduce their sending rates. In the absence of some mechanism for requiring that each host bear its share of the burden for reducing congestion, each host has the incentives to free ride on the efforts of others.

Finally, the engineering community has long recognized that because routers in the network tend to allocate bandwidth on a per-session basis, a particular end user can obtain a greater percentage of the available bandwidth simply by initiating multiple TCP sessions (Nagle 1985; Braden et al. 1998; Minar and Hedlund 1999). As the success of the Netscape browser demonstrated, opening multiple sessions can radically improve application performance. Because this strategy is subject to abuse, norms have developed requiring that any particular application initiate no more than ten to fifteen TCP sessions. Many applications ignore these limits. The most notorious offenders in this regard tend to be peer-to-peer file-sharing programs, such as BitTorrent, which can open as many as one hundred TCP sessions at a time.

The problem is that the current system for managing congestion creates a mismatch between the interests of individual end users and the interests of the network as a whole. In the words of Floyd and Fall (1999), "In the current architecture, there are no concrete incentives for individual users to use end-to-end congestion control, and there are, in some cases, 'rewards' for users that do *not* use it (i.e., they might receive a larger fraction of the link bandwidth than they would otherwise)." The problem is demonstrated by the comments of BitTorrent inventor Bram Cohen. When asked about his application problematically consuming a disproportionate amount of the bandwidth, he simply replied, "Why should I care?" (Downs 2008). As a result, the norm-based regime of informal governance, reliant on social incentives to ensure compliance, is breaking down. Again, in the words of Floyd and Fall (1999), "The Internet is no longer a small, closely knit user community, and it is no longer practical to rely on all end nodes to use end-to-end congestion control for best-effort traffic."

In short, the radical expansion in the number of Internet users since the mid-1990s has undermined the network's ability to rely on informal governance mechanisms to manage congestion. This problem will become more acute as video and other traffic associated with protocols that do not use acknowledgments become an increasingly large proportion of network traffic.

7

The Migration of Functions into the Core of the Network

The shift in the nature of end users, applications, technologies, and business relationships described above is also transforming the optimal location where certain network functions are performed. Ever since the path-breaking work of Saltzer, Reed, and Clark (1984) laid out the "end-to-end argument," the conventional wisdom has held that higher-order functions should generally be performed by hosts attached to the edge of the network rather than by routers and other elements operating in the network's core. Many policy advocates have embraced this edge-oriented approach to network design, calling it one of the Internet's defining principles and clamoring for government intervention to prevent any deviations from it (Berman and Weitzner 1995; Lessig 2001; van Schewick 2010).

I have elsewhere discussed the problems implicit with turning this particular engineering principle into a regulatory mandate and need not repeat myself here (Yoo 2004). For the purposes of this book, I prefer to focus on how the increasing diversity of end users, applications, technologies, and business relationships weakens the scope of the end-to-end argument. As discussed at length in chapter 6, the number and heterogeneity of the user base renders untenable any continued reliance on end-user cooperative behavior. In this chapter, we explore two case studies that focus on network security and congestion management so as to illustrate other forces that are causing certain host-operating functions to shift from the edge of the network to its core. Indeed, the magnitude of the changes in the technological and economic environment surrounding the Internet since the mid-1990s has led one of the authors of the original article on the end-to-end argument to reevaluate and refine his position (Blumenthal and Clark 2001; Clark and Blumenthal 2011).[12]

Network Security

As we discussed previously, regarding secure data transmission, the original article on the end-to-end argument asserted that security was the responsibility of the end node rather than the network (Bradner 2006). Consistent with that view, in the initial paradigm security was provided by a firewall and virus protection running on the end users' PCs.[13] Such an approach made sense, given the conditions that prevailed in the mid-1990s. Since that time, however, a number of other pressures have emerged on security protection, pushing it to migrate from the network's edge into its core.

One major driver of this migration is the dramatic change in the nature of the population of end users. As discussed in chapter 6, as the number of end users escalates and the Internet community becomes more diffuse, trust decreases. As illustrated by the torrent of spam following Canter and Siegel's notorious green-card advertisement, the increase in end users has reduced their ability to police themselves and has caused many of them to look to the network to curb such abuses.

Since the mid-1990s, the network has witnessed other changes as well. The advent of the Internet as a mass-market phenomenon necessarily meant that the average end user was much less technically sophisticated and received less institutional support than had previously been the case. The typical Internet user after the mid-1990s is less sophisticated than the first adopters and, hence, less capable of implementing security solutions him- or herself; this user would rather that many of these functions be performed by the network itself (Blumenthal and Clark 2001; Clark et al. 2003).

Moving functions to the network's core can reduce cost, since the network will be able to identify and discard malicious traffic early, before

---

[12] The two other authors still adhere to the original conception of end-to-end. See Saltzer 1999 and Reed 2000.

[13] See, e.g., Reno v. ACLU 1997; see also Ashcroft v. ACLU 2004, which offers a more recent reaffirmation of the edge-based vision of filtering.

it is forced to incur the expense of temporary storage and transmission to its destination. The fact that edge-based solutions must be deployed and maintained in many more locations means that network-based security protection can also be cheaper to install and update.

In addition, in what Clark and Blumenthal (2011) call "the ultimate insult," many end nodes are so infected with malware that end users can no longer trust them. As a result, end users tend to put greater trust in security services provided by third parties operating elsewhere in the network than in security services performed by their own computer.

Finally, the network may have access to more complete information than the end node. Some security solutions require access to more information than is typically available to any single end user. For example, many spam filters work best if they can search e-mail going to many different end users to try to identify characteristic patterns. Similarly, *botnet detection* functions best when examining a large number of users. A botnet is a collection of multiple computers that have been infected with malicious software, allowing them to receive commands from a bot master, usually to send spam, launch distributed denial-of-service attacks, engage in click fraud, or perform other illicit functions. Network engineers attempt to detect botnets by looking for suspicious patterns in DNS queries, attempting to identify large numbers of requests to a particular location that cannot be explained by legitimate reasons. This solution can only be implemented by an actor in a position to see the DNS-query lookups of a large number of end users and so cannot be implemented effectively by a single end node operating by itself.

All of these considerations are shifting security functions previously performed by end nodes to the network's core. Indeed, many network providers now include antivirus and firewall protection as part of the software packages used to access their systems. They are also building spam and malware filters to screen traffic as it passes through their networks.

Congestion Management

Since the mid-1990s, the changes to the technological and economic environment surrounding the Internet have also led the core of the network to play a larger role in managing congestion. As noted in chapter 3, the precipitating event was a series of "congestion collapses" during the late 1980s that slowed the network to a crawl. Jacobson (1988) devised an ingenious solution to the data-transfer gridlock, assigning responsibility for congestion management to the computers operating at the edge of the network. Notably, in making his initial proposal Jacobson recognized that this edge-based solution was incomplete and acknowledged that the core of the network would have to play a greater role.

The reasons for this shift from the network's edge to its core are easy enough to understand: It is impossible to determine one end user's impact on network congestion without knowing what the other end users are doing at the same time. Even end users that use very little bandwidth can cause a great deal of congestion if they happen to operate only at times of peak usage. Conversely, end users that consume a great deal of network capacity may contribute very little to network congestion if they operate only during the wee hours of the morning when few others are using the network.

Furthermore, as noted previously, the growth and increased usage of IP video have increased the percentage of Internet traffic consisting of UDP-based flows, which do not respond to congestion management. In addition, end users have the incentive to seize a greater percentage of the available bandwidth either by starting an excessive number of TCP sessions or by refusing to curtail usage when encountering congestion. The increasing size and heterogeneity of Internet users weaken the success of relying on end users to moderate their own behavior and heighten the need for the network to protect itself by deploying core-based congestion-management techniques.

It is for these reasons that Jacobson (1988) recognized that "only in gateways, at the convergence of flows, is there enough information to control sharing and fair allocation" and argued that router-based congestion detection was "the next big step." The IETF standard describing a now universally accepted system of active queue management known as *Random Early Discard* (RED) similarly recognizes that "it will be important for the network to be able to protect itself against unresponsive flows, and mechanisms to accomplish this must be developed and deployed" (Braden et al. 1998). Floyd and Fall (1999) sound a similar note: "Because users in the Internet do not have information about other users against whom they are competing for scarce bandwidth, the incentive mechanisms [to encourage cooperative behavior] cannot come from the other users, but would have to come from the network infrastructure itself."

In short, the engineering community has long recognized that, like network security, congestion management is a function that under many circumstances is best performed by the core of the network rather than the edge. Moreover, the types of changes that have transformed the Internet since the mid-1990s are precisely the types of changes that would cause that transformation to occur.

8

The Growing Complexity
of Internet Pricing

Changes in the technological and economic environment surrounding
the Internet over the past fifteen-plus years have also led to an increasing
diversity of pricing relationships. When the Internet first emerged, pricing was dominated by three fairly simple relationships (figure 8-1):

- First, end users typically enjoyed what is commonly known as
  flat-rate or *all-you-can-eat pricing*, in which they paid a fixed
  amount for monthly service regardless of how much bandwidth they consumed. Within certain broad limits, the amount
  paid did not vary regardless of heavy or minimal usage.

- Most other network actors connect to the Internet through a
  pricing regime known as *transit*, in which the network charges
  its customers based on the amount of bandwidth used. Transit customers agree in advance to pay for a predetermined
  amount of bandwidth (known as the *committed rate*) and
  pay incrementally for any amounts consumed above the predetermined threshold.[14]

---

[14] The amount of bandwidth consumed is typically measured not by a customer's total bandwidth
usage but, rather, by its peak bandwidth usage. To determine the size of the peak, networks typically
divide a thirty-day billing cycle into five-minute increments and calculate the utilization rate in bits
used per second for each interval, which for a thirty-day billing cycle would include 8,640 intervals.
To avoid penalizing customer for the fact that Internet traffic often arrives in brief but very intense
bursts, and to reflect the fact that individual customers' traffic bursts occur at different times, transit
pricing disregards the top 5 percent of these intervals (in effect ignoring the heaviest thirty-six hours
or 432 intervals of usage). Because this regime ignores the top 5 percent of usage, it is often called
95th percentile billing.

FIGURE 8-1
TRANSIT, PEERING, AND FLAT-RATE PRICING

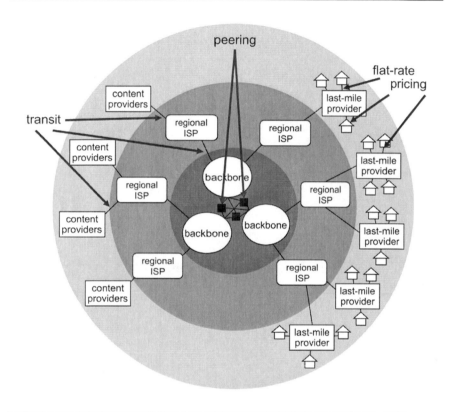

SOURCE: Author's illustration.

- Backbones typically interconnect through a pricing regime known as *peering*. They discovered that when the volume of traffic passing in each direction was roughly equal, the charges they paid essentially offset each other. When that is the case, the networks can avoid the costs of keeping track of and billing each other for the volume passing in each direction by exchanging traffic on a settlement-free basis in which they forgo paying each other anything. In order to ensure that they enter into peering arrangements only when the payments would roughly balance each other out, backbones peer only with networks of comparable size and both originate and terminate traffic.

Even when pricing relationships were relatively homogeneous, before the mid-1990s, similarly situated actors often paid widely disparate prices. Indeed, such an outcome would have been inevitable in a network consisting of thirty-five thousand autonomous systems negotiating interconnection relationships through arms-length transactions. Moreover, the standardization of these pricing relationships reflected the relative uniformity of the technological and economic environment of the time. But as the players, technologies, and business relationships have since diversified, industry actors have begun to enter into a much broader array of pricing relationships.

Deviations from Flat-Rate Pricing for End Users

Consider first the impact of increased end-user heterogeneity on flat-rate pricing. A network provider charging flat-rate prices would naturally base that price on the amount of bandwidth consumed by the average user. Such an approach worked well when end users were fairly uniform and used the network to run similar applications and to access similar content.

Flat-rate pricing becomes less effective, however, as soon as the bandwidth consumed begins to vary widely. At that point, heavier consumers enjoy a windfall, receiving services that are worth far more than the amount that they paid. Conversely, meager consumers are forced to pay more than the services are actually worth. In effect, flat-rate pricing requires low-volume users to cross-subsidize the consumption of high-volume users. Thus, flat-rate pricing becomes increasingly unfair as the amount of bandwidth consumed varies.

The emergence of bandwidth-intensive applications, such as IP video and peer-to-peer file sharing, means that certain users consume far more bandwidth than others. In fact, published reports indicate that a mere 5 percent of end users consume roughly 50 percent of total network capacity (Levy 2008; Kim 2008; Welch 2009; Canon 2009). As bandwidth consumption increasingly fluctuates wildly, flat-rate pricing becomes less and less tenable.

In addition, flat-rate pricing tends to lead to excessively high levels of network utilization. Society is best off when end users increase network usage only when the benefits they derive exceed the costs. The problem is that when end users pay flat-rate pricing they effectively pay nothing for any increases in their network usage regardless of the augmented congestion costs borne by the network as a whole. As a result, flat-rate pricing induces end users to increase their usage even when increased congestion costs outweigh the benefits enjoyed. Put a different way, under flat-rate pricing, congestion represents an externality that allows end users to force others to bear the congestion costs created by any increases in their network usage. Flat-rate pricing does not force end users to bear the full costs of their behavior, which then gives end users the systematic incentive to increase their network usage beyond levels most beneficial to society as a whole (Yoo 2006).

The classic solution is to scale cost to usage—that is, to set the price for using the congestible resource exactly equal to the congestion costs that the end user is imposing on other users. Setting prices in this manner would give end users the incentive to use the network only when the benefits they derive from doing so would exceed the total costs of their doing so. This is why most economists regard flat-rate pricing of the Internet to be a public policy anomaly.[15]

Compelling reasons exist, therefore, for moving beyond flat-rate pricing. Unfortunately, this is far easier said than done. Consider first the fact that congestion arises only when particular network elements approach saturation. This means that proper congestion pricing depends as much on accurately timing when consumption will reach capacity as it does on the amount of bandwidth consumed. End users who consume large amounts of bandwidth may in fact cause very little congestion if they operate only during hours when the network is slack. Conversely, end users who consume only small amounts of bandwidth may nonetheless significantly increase congestion if they use the network during peak

---

[15] For classic statements of this position, see Coase 1946 and Berglas 1976. For applications to the Internet, see Kahn 2006b and Yoo 2006.

FIGURE 8-2

INEFFICIENCIES OF PEAK-LOAD PRICING

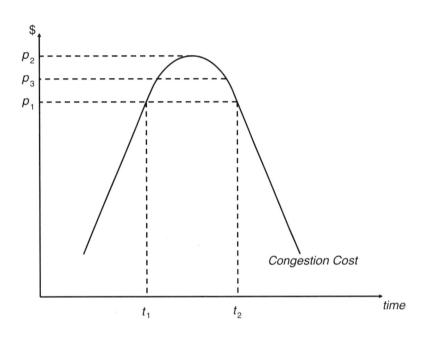

SOURCE: Yoo 2008.

periods, when network elements are close to saturation. This in turn
implies the following: Pricing that prevents each end user from imposing
congestion costs on other users should vary from location to location,
depending on which areas of the network are currently congested. These
variations are likely to be particularly severe for technologies that are
more susceptible to local congestion—like cable modem and wireless
broadband systems—than for wireline technologies. In addition, those
prices should vary dynamically over the course of the entire day.

The problem is that consumers find it difficult to deal with prices
that vary this rapidly in terms of time and space. Studies suggest that

consumers can only deal effectively with a limited number of pricing periods over the course of a single day (Park and Mitchell 1987).[16] So instead of having usage prices that vary dynamically minute by minute, most network providers divide the day into different time periods and charge different prices based on when the end user is using the network. (Classic examples include free night and weekend minutes on mobile phones and evening and night rates for long-distance telephone calls.)

However, basing prices on different time periods mimics congestion-based pricing imperfectly. At times it will overdeter network consumption, while at other times it will underdeter network consumption (Yoo 2008). Consider, for example, the pricing scheme represented in figure 8-2, in which the time of day is represented on the horizontal axis and the congestion cost at any particular time is represented on the vertical axis. What price should the network charge during the interval between t_1 and t_2, the busiest time of the day?

Any uniform price charged during this period will result in a degree of inefficiency. If the network sets its price at the lowest congestion cost during this period (represented by p_1), the price will consistently fall below the congestion costs of network usage. As a result, pricing at p_1 will cause end users to increase their network usage even when it is socially inefficient for them to do so. If the network instead sets its price at the highest congestion cost during this period (represented by p_2), the price will consistently exceed the congestion costs, which in turn causes end users to curtail their network usage even when increasing network usage would create benefits that exceed congestion costs. If the network sets the price somewhere in between the two (represented by p_3), end users will be overdeterred during the beginning and concluding portions of the pricing period while being undeterred during the middle.

In addition, the end users' natural responses to the imposition of higher prices during some portion of the day would be to shift some of their usage to other time periods. This redistribution of calling patterns creates "shoulders" in the distribution of traffic that increase congestion immediately before and after the period of higher prices. As a result,

---

[16] Indeed, a growing body of research suggests that consumers prefer flat-rate pricing even when it would be more expensive (Train 1994; Mitomo 2001).

networks trying to charge higher prices during peak times typically must also charge intermediate prices (sometimes called *shoulder rates*) during the time period immediately preceding and following the peak-load period. Inducing people to alter their calling patterns necessarily harms consumers, as it forces them away from their preferred calling patterns. In setting near-peak prices, regulators would face the welfare losses discussed above that arise with setting peak prices.

The difficulty in deploying peak-load pricing in a way that actually benefits consumers is demonstrated eloquently by the failure of telephone companies' previous attempts to deploy congestion pricing for local telephone service. The imperfections inherent in implementing congestion pricing ended up offsetting all of the expected efficiency gains (Mitchell 1978; Perl 1985; Park and Mitchell 1987). The fact that wireless telephone providers are moving away from metered pricing to charging fixed prices for buckets of minutes or even deploying all-you-can-eat pricing further attests to the difficulty of deploying congestion pricing.

And the difficulties inherent in determining an efficient pricing structure are compounded by the fact that Internet congestion arises only when network elements approach saturation. This means that proper congestion pricing depends as much on the timing of when the end user is consuming capacity as it does on the total amount of bandwidth consumed. End users who consume large amounts of bandwidth may in fact cause very little congestion if they do so only during hours when the network is slack. Conversely, end users who consume only small amounts of bandwidth may nonetheless be responsible for a significant increase in congestion if they use the network during peak periods when network elements are close to saturation. As a result, network providers cannot implement proper congestion pricing simply by metering bandwidth usage. Instead, congestion management necessitates focusing not on total bandwidth usage but rather solely on peak usage. And even then one end user's peak bandwidth usage will not cause congestion unless it coincides with other end users' peaks. Thus end users cannot individually determine the impact their flows are having on network congestion. Rather, this can only be determined by also looking at the flows that other end users are introducing into the network on a dynamic basis that assesses the level of congestion in different parts of the network.

Setting proper congestion pricing is complicated further by the fact that any network connection will only perform as well as the least congested network element in the transmission path. The Internet, however, is an amalgam of thirty-five thousand autonomous systems that hand off traffic without knowing anything about the network conditions downstream. The fact that each system only has localized knowledge about the conditions within its own network (or at most limited information about the conditions in adjacent networks) means that no actor in the system is likely to have sufficient information to make the necessary optimization decision. The closest approximation the network can make in the face of this limited information is to charge an admission price at the edge of the network that is at best a rough proxy for the actual congestion conditions in the network's core (Shenker et al. 1996).

Therefore, even though the emerging consensus recognizes the need to move away from flat-rate end-user pricing, industry actors are still struggling to determine exactly how the new pricing regime should be structured. It thus comes as no surprise that they are experimenting with a wide variety of new pricing arrangements.

The Importance of Investment Incentives and the Insights of Ramsey Pricing

Another force driving the Internet toward more complex pricing regimes is the number of differences between the last generation and the current generation of broadband technologies. As noted in chapter 4, the first wave of broadband deployment focused on cable modem and DSL systems. Because these technologies leveraged investments in existing technologies, they only required roughly $400 to $800 per customer to deploy. The relatively modest size of these investments allowed network providers a reasonable return on investment with only modest price increases that were in turn an easy sell to consumers, who found the dramatic increase in bandwidth to be very attractive.

The second—and current—wave of broadband deployment is quite different. Rather than leveraging existing technologies, fiber-to-the-home, fourth-generation wireless, and other technologies on which the current round of bandwidth expansion is based require new investments that are considerably more expensive. As noted earlier, the cost of deploying Verizon's FiOS network may run as high as $4,000 per subscriber. Consistent with that, estimates of how much it would take to deliver 100 Mbps to 100 million households typically run in the neighborhood of $350 to $400 billion.

Most industry and political observers believe that the federal government will not be in a position to allocate that amount of money to upgrade our nation's broadband infrastructure for the foreseeable future. The next-generation network will thus be built by private enterprise. But private corporations cannot be expected to undertake such investments unless they have a reasonable prospect of recovering their upfront costs from consumers who are using the increased bandwidth and other enhancements to the existing network. Unless they receive additional revenue from their investments to upgrade the network, they will have no incentive to invest in the first place. In short, enhanced services cost money. Logically, then, consumers who expect to benefit from those enhanced services should expect to cover their share of the costs of providing those services.

One solution would be to recover the costs of upgrading the network by charging a uniform price to all Internet users, and this uniform price would necessarily be higher than the uniform price charged before the network upgrade. Not everyone, however, needs those enhanced services. Many Americans, for example, are primarily e-mail users who are perfectly happy with the quality of the network as it exists today. Charging higher prices to end users who do not need the additional services is simultaneously uneconomical and unfair. What makes more sense is to finance the network upgrade through a system of tiered prices that places the burden of the upgrade on those end users who actually benefit from it without forcing those who are happy with the existing, limited network service to pay more.

Stated somewhat more formally, the trend away from flat-rate pricing is better understood when considering the longstanding device known as *Ramsey pricing*.[17] One of the challenges with setting prices in network

---

[17] Ramsey (1927) first articulated this principle in the context of taxation. Baumol and Bradford (1970) extended these principles to regulatory pricing. For an application to the Internet, see Yoo 2006.

industries is that service providers cannot include only the incremental cost of providing service (which economists call *marginal cost*). Rather, prices must also include a portion of the upfront, fixed cost of establishing the network in the first place. The problem is that setting prices that exceed marginal cost causes people to curtail their consumption below efficient levels. The higher the price increase above marginal cost, the greater the welfare loss to society.

Ramsey pricing takes advantage of the fact that consumers vary in terms of their sensitivity to price changes (which economists call *price elasticity*). Some consumers are price insensitive, in that they need certain products so badly that they will continue to purchase those products even if prices increase sharply. Others are very price sensitive, in that any increase in price causes them to curtail their consumption sharply. Ramsey realized that every customer need not bear the same proportion of the fixed cost. Indeed, a producer could minimize the reduction in demand simply by allocating a greater proportion of the fixed cost on those who are the least price sensitive while allocating a smaller proportion to those who are the most price sensitive. Allocating the fixed-cost markup in this manner minimizes the falloff in demand associated with charging prices that exceed marginal cost. Indeed, if fixed costs are allocated in precise inverse proportion to the elasticity of demand, Ramsey pricing can achieve the perfectly competitive result.

As a result, economists have long embraced Ramsey pricing as a way to maximize social welfare and make it easier for networks to recover the large, upfront investments needed to establish networks in the first place (Scherer and Ross 1990; Laffont and Tirole 2000; Viscusi, Harrington, and Vernon 2005). It thus represents another consideration driving the Internet away from flat-rate pricing and a strong justification for forgoing regulatory price-setting so that individual producers can experiment with different pricing regimes in a decentralized manner.

The Impact of Peer-to-Peer Applications on End-User Pricing

Another often overlooked change driving the industry away from flat-rate pricing is the advent of peer-to-peer technologies. As an initial matter, peer-to-peer applications are particularly problematic in that they consist of machine-to-machine communications. For applications that require a human being to initiate them, the number of hours that the end user is physically at her machine places a natural limit on the amount of bandwidth that end user can consume. But bandwidth consumption is not self-limiting in this manner when communications are machine-to-machine, meaning that applications involving machine-to-machine communication use network resources much more intensively than other applications.

Moreover, as discussed in chapter 3, the Internet of the mid-1990s was designed around a client-server architecture, in which computers that were connected to the edge of the network consisted either of end users (clients) who submitted requests for content or of servers that hosted and delivered content to those end users on request. Interestingly, the pricing mechanisms that were initially employed ensured that the compensation received by network providers roughly reflected the burden that particular traffic was placing on the network. Although the end users typically paid flat-rate prices, the servers typically paid transit prices, which increased with the peak amount of bandwidth used. As a result, one hundred requests for a seven hundred megabyte movie would generate seventy gigabytes of traffic from the server, which would then result in higher transit prices paid by the content owner.

The calculus is rather different under peer-to-peer architectures. A movie could initially be downloaded just once from the server. The subsequent ninety-nine requests for the movie could then be served by other end users running the same peer-to-peer software. Although the server hosting the movie in a client-server architecture connects to the network through a transit arrangement that increases with the peak amount of bandwidth consumed, the peers that support a peer-to-peer architecture typically only pay a flat rate that is not usage sensitive. The growing importance of peer-to-peer architectures means that downloads that used to be charged usage-sensitive pricing are being replaced by downloads subject to flat-rate pricing. The result is that the total amount paid to support the one hundred downloads will be less likely to reflect the true burden that those downloads place on the network (Yoo 2010c). The obvious solution is for last-mile providers to abandon flat-rate pricing and instead impose some type of volume-sensitive pricing.

Paid Peering and the Economics of Two-Sided Markets

In addition to altering the dynamics surrounding end user pricing, the changes to the Internet since the mid-1990s have placed pressure on the backbone-to-backbone pricing relationship called *peering*. As noted above, backbones exchange traffic on a settlement-free basis in which no money changes hands. In effect, peering means that backbones do not receive any compensation for terminating traffic arriving from the other network, even though they must incur significant costs for terminating that traffic. The rationale is simple: if the flows passing in each direction are roughly equal, any payments passing in one direction would offset the payments passing in the other direction. Peering allows both backbones to avoid the costs of metering and billing for traffic.

Although some scholars wrongly refer to this as *zero-price interconnection*, it is better understood as a form of barter, since it is in effect an in-kind exchange that depends on the value on each side of the transaction being roughly equal. For peering to be sensible for both parties, however, two things must be true. First, the costs of terminating traffic must be symmetrical on both sides of the peering point. Second, the revenue generated on both sides of the peering point must also be roughly equal. If either proposition does not hold, the flows passing in each direction will no longer be of the same economic significance, because one side either faces higher costs or derives lower benefits than the other side. Regardless of whether the imbalance results from cost or revenue asymmetries, when value is no longer equal on both sides of the transaction, barter no longer makes sense.

The way that the Internet has evolved since the mid-1990s has undermined both of these presuppositions. As the Internet has matured, two distinctly different types of networks have emerged. One type, sometimes called *content* networks, focuses on providing connectivity to content and application providers. The other type, sometimes called *eyeball* networks, focuses on providing connectivity to end users.

Examining first the cost side, content and eyeball networks face widely divergent cost structures. The costs of operating a content network are generally quite low, typically requiring only a single high-speed line from the content/application provider's location to a network access point.

Moreover, content networks' customers also typically possess sufficient scale to permit content networks to deploy high-volume equipment, which in turn reduces unit costs dramatically. In contrast, the costs of operating an eyeball network are much higher. Unlike content networks, which only need to connect one location to another in order to provide service, eyeball networks must bear the expense of laying networks of wires that blanket entire residential neighborhoods. This radical asymmetry in cost would lead one to expect that peering partners predominantly serving eyeball networks would not accept exchanging equally sized traffic on a settlement-free basis, since the differences in cost would cause the value of their side of the barter exchange to be much lower than the value on the other side.

Content and eyeball networks have grown increasingly divergent in terms of revenue. Advertising has become the Internet's most important source of revenue. The complication is that advertising revenue flows primarily to content providers. As a result, parties on the content-network side of the peering point derive more value from the traffic than do the parties on the eyeball-network side. Again, even though the size of the traffic is roughly equal, the value is sufficiently divergent to undermine the case for barter.

When costs and value are asymmetrical, using barter to exchange traffic on a settlement-free basis no longer makes sense. Instead, the literature on two-sided markets indicates that society would be better off if the side of the transaction incurring lower costs and deriving more revenue from the network were to make a side payment to the side of the transaction that faces higher costs and lower revenue. Moreover, one would expect the specific prices paid to vary from provider to provider and to change dynamically over time. Under appropriate circumstances, one might even expect the direction of the payments to reverse (Yoo 2008 and 2009).

These dynamics are illustrated vividly by the history of the broadcast television industry. Like content networks on the Internet, broadcast networks aggregate program content and distribute it (via satellite) to individual cities for local distribution. Furthermore, local television stations serve the same functions as cable modem and DSL providers on the Internet, distributing that content from a central location in a city to individual homes. As is the case with the Internet, the costs are radically asymmetric in broadcast television, with the costs of national distribution totaling far less than the costs of local distribution. As is the case with the Internet, revenue primarily derives from advertising, with the lion's share flowing to the content networks instead of the eyeball networks.

Historically, these cost and revenue differentials have led these parties away from interconnecting on a settlement-free basis. Instead, for decades the standard business arrangement has been for television networks to subsidize the operations of local broadcast stations by paying them to be members of their television networks. The broadcast television industry's revenue and cost structure make such arrangements quite logical. As with the Internet, the per-unit distribution costs faced by eyeball networks (local television stations) are much higher than the costs of distributing the content networks (broadcast television networks). More importantly, the broadcast networks are the primary beneficiaries of advertising revenue, and the cost of paying these broadcast stations to affiliate with their network is more than offset by the increase in advertising revenue made possible by the fact that the network is now able to reach a larger audience. Broadcast television thus illustrates how firms operating on one side of the market might find it economically beneficial to subsidize end users on the other side of the market.

Furthermore, the magnitude of the affiliation fees that the networks pay to broadcast stations is anything but uniform. The precise amount varies with the relative strength of the network and the relative strength of the broadcast station. Stronger broadcast stations receive more, while weaker ones receive less. Equally interesting is the fact that in recent years the cash flow has begun to vary in its direction as well as magnitude, with weaker stations having to pay rather than be paid to be part of a television network. The dynamic nature of this pricing regime benefits consumers by providing incentives for networks to invest in better quality programming and provide better carriage.

This analysis reveals the problems with the claim that allowing network providers to charge content and application providers for premium services would force consumers to pay twice. As a general matter, pricing flexibility makes it easier for network providers to recover the costs of building additional bandwidth. Left to their own devices, network providers would set prices designed to maximize the revenue generated by each side of the market. So long as competitive entry is sufficiently feasible to prevent network providers from simply pocketing the extra returns, facilitating the ability of network providers to generate revenue from one side of the market will reduce the proportion of the fixed costs that the network provider will have to recover from the other side of the market. Thus, granting network providers pricing flexibility with respect to content and application providers should reduce the economic burden borne by end users.

Conversely, preventing network providers from exercising pricing flexibility with respect to content and application providers while permitting them to exercise pricing flexibility against end users simply increases the proportion of the cost that network providers must recover directly from end users. This simultaneously raises the prices paid by consumers and decreases the likelihood that the capital improvements will ever be made (Moffett 2006). Conversely, enhancing pricing flexibility on both sides of the market increases the likelihood that network providers will recover a greater proportion of the costs of upgrading the network from content and application providers. Charging content and application providers premium prices for premium services is thus a way to reduce, not increase, the burden borne by consumers.

This is not to say that allowing network providers to offer multiple classes of service would always be economically beneficial. If perfect price discrimination were feasible, differential pricing schemes would always benefit society. Perfect price discrimination is impossible, however, and to the extent that price discrimination is imperfect, the practice might reduce as well as increase economic welfare. That said, economic textbooks generally conclude that imperfect price discrimination is more likely to be beneficial than not (Lipsey, Steiner, and Purvis 1987; Scherer and Ross 1990). In any event, the real possibility that pricing flexibility may benefit and not just harm consumers counsels strongly against erecting a categorical ban against the practice and provides an important consideration that a well designed case-by-case approach should take into account.

The Benefits of Permitting Greater Variety in Pricing Relationships

The changes discussed above are also likely to make Internet pricing become more varied and complex. Such a development ought to be embraced rather than resisted. Price mechanisms are essential for signaling the extent to which markets are in short-run disequilibrium and for providing the incentive to reallocate resources in a more efficient manner. Prices also provide the incentive to upgrade existing networks and to invest in new network technologies. Allowing different actors to pursue different pricing strategies decentralizes decision making and encourages experiments with a wide variety of pricing relationships that each compensate for the difficulties in establishing true congestion-based pricing in different ways.

Pricing flexibility is the standard mechanism by which our society rewards socially beneficial behavior and reallocates resources. This process of equilibration works well so long as entry barriers are relatively low and inputs are relatively mobile. These conditions are easily met with respect to content and applications, which are already very competitive and unprotected by entry barriers (and therefore likely to remain that way). The upsurge of mobile wireless as a last-mile platform has made these conditions easier to satisfy on the network provider side as well. The impending deployment of WiMax, LTE, and other technologies promises to open the last mile to competition still further in the future.

Interestingly, even though many new business arrangements are criticized as attempts for existing players to exercise monopoly power, the increasing diversity of business relationships and pricing regimes often serves to weaken rather than strengthen market power. Additionally, moving away from the hierarchical nature of the previous regime makes the network more robust against system failure.

Technological solutions are complicated by the fact that the Internet is comprised of numerous autonomous actors whose actions can be hard to coordinate. The lack of coordination raises the real danger of strategic behavior. Indeed, the recent dispute between Comcast and BitTorrent can be understood as a struggle over whether optimization of traffic patterns in light of congestion will occur at the network level or the application level.

9

The Inevitability of Intermediation

Many observers anticipated that by enabling every individual to communicate directly with all other individuals, the Internet would flatten all human relations in ways that would completely eliminate the power of all intermediaries. Economically, some predicted that enhancing communication would undermine the power of all wholesalers and market makers and instead allow people to buy directly from manufacturers (Malone, Yates, and Benjamin 1987; Benjamin and Wigand 1995). Other commentators from across the political spectrum optimistically argued that the Internet would allow speakers to bypass the established media companies that have long played a gatekeeper function in content markets and instead to speak directly to audiences (Volokh 1995; Lessig 2001). Perhaps the most sweeping statement in this regard was offered by the Supreme Court in *Reno v. ACLU* (1997), which lauded how the Internet empowers "any person with a phone line" to become a "pamphleteer" or a "town crier with a voice that resonates farther than it could from any soapbox." Some public-interest advocates have gone even farther, holding up complete disintermediation as the epitome of free speech and calling on the federal government to adopt regulations to effectuate it.

Over time, such claims about complete disintermediation have proven to be unduly utopian. On the economic side, the advent of the Internet did not abolish wholesaling as an institution. Scholars studying this phenomenon have gained a better appreciation of the functions that intermediaries serve in facilitating economic transactions (Sarkar, Butler, and Steinfeld 1995; Downes and Mui 1998; Scott 2000; Cotter 2006). We have already discussed in chapter 7 how intermediaries operating in the core of the network continue to play key roles in providing network security and in managing network congestion.

In this chapter we explore the ongoing roles intermediaries continue to play in content markets during the Internet era.[18] In particular, we review the functions that speech intermediaries continue to play in the Internet, including the manner in which they help end users organize economic transactions and manage the daily barrage of wanted and unwanted content.

Their role is noted by the Supreme Court's First Amendment jurisprudence, which recognizes that exercises of editorial discretion promote rather than detract from free-speech values. Indeed, the Supreme Court's precedents regard intermediaries' editorial discretion as inviolate even if the intermediary enjoys monopoly power or acts as a private censor. The Court has recognized a small number of exceptions to justify some limits on intermediaries' editorial discretion in broadcast and cable television. These exceptions have come under broad analytical attack, which has undercut their viability. Moreover, the courts have already found them inapplicable to the Internet.

These decisions suggest that we ought to view the exercise of editorial discretion by intermediaries as promoting rather than denigrating free-speech values. In any event, these exercises of editorial discretion are inevitable, which in turn means that any notion of an unintermediated Internet where speakers speak directly to audiences without passing through any gatekeepers is and has always been more myth than reality. The real question is not *whether* some actor will serve as intermediary but, rather, *which* actor. Together these insights demonstrate that intermediation ought not be regarded as a necessary evil, as some commentators have suggested. On the contrary, intermediation can play a key role in helping end users obtain access to the content and applications they desire.

The Benefits of Intermediation

Many of the advantages consumers enjoy because of intermediation are economic benefits. As noted in chapter 7, the performance of certain functions, such as congestion management, require information about the

---

[18] For a more in-depth analysis of these issues, see Yoo 2010b.

flows that multiple end users are introducing into the network. Because end users typically lack sufficient information to perform this function on their own, complex congestion management depends on some intermediary in a position to see the flows of multiple end users. Effective economic performance on the network is also inhibited by certain structural features, such as asymmetric information, that lead individual end users to act strategically in ways that can prevent the network from realizing welfare maximizing outcomes. When that is the case, the optimal economic outcome may depend on the presence of an intermediary in a position to compensate for this strategic behavior (Yoo 2010b and 2010c).

In addition, rather than storing content in a single location, the Internet is increasingly employing systems that store content in multiple locations and access them dynamically depending on network conditions. Prominent examples include peer-to-peer networks and CDNs. Determining from which particular location to serve any particular request can only be made by an intermediary in a position to direct such requests in a sensible manner.

More importantly, intermediaries play a key role in helping end users cope with the deluge of content that inundates end users every day. As discussed in chapters 6 and 7, intermediaries play a key role in shielding end users from unwanted content. Indeed, because network security often requires aggregating information across many end users, individual end users may be inherently unable to perform these functions themselves.

And perhaps more important still, intermediaries help end users locate and obtain access to content they find desirable. Since the mid-1990s, the Internet has developed into a vast and vibrant source of media content that grows larger with every passing day. The increasing importance of user-generated content (through the applications associated with Web 2.0) has caused both the volume and the variability in the quality of online content to increase dramatically.

Simply put, individual end users cannot be expected to crawl through the onslaught of new and existing content that appears on the Internet without the help of filters. It is inevitable that end users will rely on a wide variety of content aggregators, including e-mail bulletins, bloggers, and search engines, to help identify and obtain access to fresh content relevant to their interests. Moreover, intermediaries are able to maximize the value of their efforts to sort through this information by providing the same information to multiple customers. That said, the approach taken by each intermediary varies; indeed, it is the very difference in editorial discretion exercised by these intermediaries that make them most valuable to end users.

Perhaps the most dramatic example of this phenomenon is Google's emergence as the world's dominant search engine. Google was actually a late arrival on the scene and already faced stiff competition from AltaVista and a host of other well established search engines. Google nonetheless succeeded because it utilized an algorithm that was more effective in identifying content that end users would find interesting. Of course, Google's page ranking protocol orders results in a unique way that differs from every other search engine. Indeed, that is precisely the point. Providing more effective search results is the way the search engines compete with one another. Because each protocol is distinct, each inevitably treats some websites more favorably and other websites less favorably than other algorithms. Although such differentiation leads some websites to complain they are stuck in Google's doghouse (Nocera 2008), such differences are the inevitable byproduct of the differentiation that is the foundation of search engines' success. Conversely, forcing search engines to adhere to any particular approach or to ensure that results are ordered in a particular way would limit the primary value that search engines provide their consumers.

The Supreme Court's Embrace of Intermediation

The Supreme Court has long recognized that editors can help sort through large amounts of content. Indeed, allowing editors to exercise this power promotes rather than weakens free-speech values. Were they required to make their networks available to everyone on a nondiscriminatory basis, these same free-speech values would be compromised (Yoo 2010b).

The Court offered its most extensive discussion of these principles in *Columbia Broadcasting System, Inc. v. Democratic National Committee* (1973), in which the Court rejected claims that a broadcaster's refusal to carry an editorial advertisement violated the First Amendment. The Court began by reviewing the legislative history of the Radio Act of 1927, concluding that "Congress specifically dealt with—and firmly rejected—the argument that the broadcast facilities should be open on a nonselective basis to all persons wishing to talk about public issues." Instead, "in the area of discussion of public issues Congress chose to leave broad journalistic discretion with the licensee." Although certain members of Congress raised the concern that failure to place limits on broadcasters' editorial discretion would give them the power of "private censorship," Congress declined to limit that discretion because, in the words of the principal architect of the Radio Act of 1927, "it seemed unwise to put the broadcaster under the hampering control of being a common carrier and compelled to accept anything and everything that was offered him so long as the price was paid."

Congress reaffirmed these principles in the Communications Act of 1934. In the process, it rejected an amendment that would have required every broadcaster that presented views on a public issue up for consideration in the next election to provide equal time to those holding opposing views, arguing that enactment of such a provision "would have imposed a limited obligation on broadcasters to turn over their microphones to persons wishing to speak out on certain public issues." The Court determined that these and other decisions "evince[d] a legislative desire to preserve values of private journalism" and "to permit private broadcasting to develop with the widest journalistic freedom consistent with its public obligations." In making this commitment to editorial discretion, Congress did not ignore the possibility that broadcasters might engage in what amounts to private censorship. Although a "single person or group [could] place themselves in [a] position where they can censor the material which shall be broadcasted to the public," "Congress appears to have concluded…that of these two choices—private or official censorship—Government censorship would be the most pervasive, the most self-serving, the most difficult to restrain and hence the one most to be avoided."

The portion of the Court's opinion discussing the First Amendment espoused similar principles. The Court specifically rejected the argument that giving speakers nondiscriminatory access to broadcast networks would promote free speech, concluding that "[a]ll journalistic tradition and experience is to the contrary." The portion of the opinion that did not command a majority of the Court similarly noted that an intermediary's exercise of editorial discretion is only properly limited by its audience, not by the government: "The power of a privately owned newspaper to advance its own political, social, and economic views is bounded by only two facts: first, the acceptance of a sufficient number of readers—and hence advertisers—to assure financial success; and, second, the journalistic integrity of its editors and publishers." The plurality further concluded:

> [I]t would be anomalous for us to hold, in the name of promoting the constitutional guarantees of free expression, that the day-to-day editorial decisions of broadcast licensees are subject to the kind of restraints urged by respondents. To do so in the name of the First Amendment would be a contradiction. Journalistic discretion would in many ways be lost to the rigid limitations that the First Amendment imposes on Government.

Justice Stewart's partial concurrence similarly concluded that the First Amendment "gives every newspaper the liberty to print what it chooses and reject what it chooses, free from the intrusive editorial thumb of the Government."

In the process, the Court rejected the argument that government intervention was justified by private exercises of editorial discretion favoring certain viewpoints over others:

> For better or worse, editing is what editors are for; and editing is selection and choice of material. That editors…can and do abuse this power is beyond doubt, but that is no reason to deny the discretion Congress provided. Calculated risks of abuse are taken in order to preserve higher values. The presence of these risks is nothing new; the authors of the Bill of Rights accepted the reality that these risks were evils for which there was no acceptable remedy other than a spirit of moderation and a sense of responsibility—and civility—on the part of those who exercise the guaranteed freedoms of expression.

Justice Douglas's concurrence found no historical support for the claim that allegations of editorial bias justified regulatory intervention. After noting that Benjamin Franklin and Thomas Jefferson rejected claims that biases in exercise of editorial discretion could justify governmental intervention, Douglas concluded, "Of course there is private censorship in the newspaper field....But if the Government is the censor, administrative fiat, not freedom of choice, carries the day." Douglas continued, "Both TV and radio news broadcasts frequently tip the news one direction or another.... Yet so do the newspapers and the magazines and other segments of the press. The standards of TV, radio, newspapers, or magazines—whether of excellence or mediocrity—are beyond the reach of Government."

The Supreme Court has on numerous subsequent occasions reaffirmed that broadcasters' exercise of editorial discretion promotes free-speech values and has described it as "the absolute freedom to advocate one's own positions without also presenting opposing viewpoints" (*FCC v. League of Women Voters of California* [1984]; *Turner Broadcasting System, Inc. v. FCC* [1994]; *Arkansas Educational Television Commission v. Forbes* [1998]). While concurring in *Miami Herald Publishing Co. v. Tornillo* (1974), Justice White similarly noted:

> According to our accepted jurisprudence, the First Amendment erects a virtually insurmountable barrier between government and the print media as far as government tampering, in advance of publication, with news and editorial content is concerned. A newspaper or magazine is not a public utility subject to "reasonable" governmental regulation in matters affecting the exercise of journalistic judgment as to what shall be printed.... Regardless of how beneficent-sounding the purpose of controlling the press might be, we prefer "the power of reason as applied through public discussion" and remain intensely skeptical about those measures that would allow government to insinuate itself into the editorial rooms of this Nation's press.

The Court later recognized that the same principles apply to editorial discretion exercised by cable operators (*FCC v. Midwest Video Corp.* 1979; *City of Los Angeles v. Preferred Communications, Inc.* 1986; *Leathers v. Medlock* 1991; *Turner Broadcasting System, Inc. v. FCC* 1994; *Denver Area Educational Telecommunications Consortium v. FCC* 1996).

Over the years, the Court has recognized three exceptions that permitted some limitation to particular intermediaries' editorial discretion.[19] The first, known as the *scarcity doctrine*, justifies interfering with broadcasters' editorial discretion by requiring them to carry certain speech (*Red Lion Broadcasting Co. v. FCC* 1967; *CBS, Inc. v. FCC* 1981). The rationale behind the scarcity doctrine is that because the number of broadcast channels was strictly limited, the government necessarily had to become directly involved in allocating opportunities to speak.

The explosion of broadcast channels and other media outlets has undercut the empirical premise that broadcast programming is inherently scarce. Moreover, commentators and subsequent courts have subjected the scarcity doctrine to a scathing analytical critique that has largely undercut its viability. Most important for the purposes of this book is the fact that the Supreme Court's decision in *Reno v. ACLU* (1997) has already held the scarcity doctrine inapplicable to the Internet. Because the Internet "provides relatively unlimited, low-cost capacity for communication of all kinds," it "can hardly be considered a 'scarce' expressive commodity." As a result, the Court flatly concluded that its precedents applying the scarcity doctrine to broadcasting "provide no basis for qualifying the level of First Amendment scrutiny that should be applied to this medium."

The second exception to editorial discretion stems from *FCC v. Pacifica Foundation* (1978), which announced two new rationales for applying a lower standard of First Amendment protection to broadcasting: "First, the broadcast media have established a uniquely pervasive presence in the lives of all Americans" and act as an "intruder" that "confronts the citizen...in the privacy of the home." "Second, broadcasting is uniquely accessible to children, even those too young to read."

Like the scarcity doctrine, courts and commentators have long challenged *Pacifica*'s analytical coherence. Recent judicial decisions suggest

---

[19] For my critique, see Yoo 2003 and Forthcoming.

that the courts may be ready to abandon the doctrine with respect to broadcasting. Even if the Supreme Court declines to overrule *Pacifica* with respect to broadcasting, its opinion in *Reno v. ACLU* has already rejected attempts to extend *Pacifica* to the Internet. As the Court noted, "the Internet is not as 'invasive' as radio or television." Moreover, it analogized the Internet to its previous decision refusing to extend *Pacifica*'s "empathically narrow holding" to dial-a-porn, holding that, like dial-a-porn, the Internet "requires the listener to take affirmative steps to receive the communication." The fact that indecent content is generally preceded by warnings also makes it less likely that the recipient would be taken by surprise.

The third exception to editorial freedom stems from the Supreme Court's decision in *Turner Broadcasting System, Inc. v. FCC* (1994), which would eventually lead to the Court's upholding the must-carry statute requiring cable operators to carry all full-power local television stations for free. The Court began by declaring that there can be "no disagreement" on the "initial premise" that "[c]able programmers and cable operators engage in and transmit speech, and they are entitled to the protection of the speech and press provisions of the First Amendment." Indeed, that is the case regardless of whether the cable operator is offering "original programming" or is simply "exercising editorial discretion over which stations or programs to include in its repertoire." The Court also affirmatively rejected extending the scarcity doctrine to cable, holding that "the rationale for applying a less rigorous standard of First Amendment scrutiny to broadcast regulation, whatever its validity in the case elaborating it, does not apply in the context of cable regulation" because "cable television does not suffer from the inherent limitations that characterize the broadcast medium" and does not pose "any danger of physical interference between two cable speakers attempting to share the same channel."

Turner nonetheless declined to apply full First Amendment protection to cable, based on "an important technological difference between newspapers and cable television." Specifically, the Court noted that "[a]lthough a daily newspaper and a cable operator both may enjoy monopoly status in a given locale, the cable operator exercises far greater control over access to the relevant medium." Even if a newspaper holds a natural monopoly, it "does not possess the power to obstruct readers' access to other competing publications" and cannot "prevent other newspapers from being distributed to willing recipients in the same locale."

The Court concluded, however, that "[t]he same is not true with cable." Instead, "[w]hen an individual subscribes to cable, the physical connection between the television set and the cable network gives the cable operator *bottleneck*, or *gatekeeper*, control over most (if not all) of the television programming that is channeled into the subscriber's home" (emphasis added). Thus cable operators' "ownership of the essential pathway for cable speech" gives cable operators the power to "silence the voice of competing speakers with a mere flick of a switch." The Court ruled that this "physical control of a critical pathway of communication" creates a "potential for abuse of...private power over a central avenue of communication" and hence justifies limiting cable operators' editorial discretion in ways that would not be permitted with respect to newspapers.

The arrival of direct broadcast satellites (DBS) and the emergence of multichannel video services provided by telephone companies (such as Verizon's FiOS and AT&T's U-verse services) have raised serious doubts as to the bottleneck rationale's continuing validity with respect to cable television. In any event, judicial decisions have made clear that the bottleneck rationale almost certainly does not apply to the Internet. The courts have repeatedly recognized that cable modem and DSL systems are engaged in vibrant competition that has been recently enhanced by other technologies, such as fiber-to-the-home (like Verizon's FiOS system) and wireless broadband providers. Other new wireless technologies based on the spectrum allocated by the 700 MHz auction are waiting in the wings.

The competitiveness of the broadband industry has led courts and regulators to reject claims that just because the market for Internet service is sufficiently concentrated, it is then justifiable to subject it to mandatory access requirements. For example, in *Comcast Cablevision of Broward County, Inc. v. Broward County* (2000) the court held that the level of competition between DSL and cable modem providers rendered the bottleneck rationale of *Turner* inapplicable to cable modem service. Similarly, in *United States Telecom Association v. FCC* (2002), the court ruled that "the robust competition...in the broadband market" rendered invalid an FCC decision requiring local telephone companies to give competitive DSL providers access to the high-frequency portion of their loops. In 2005, the FCC similarly determined that last-mile broadband services had become sufficiently competitive to justify removing DSL-related components from the list of network elements to which incumbent local telephone companies had to provide unbundled access under the Telecommunications Act of 1996. Most recently, the Supreme Court specifically ruled in *Pacific Bell Telephone Co. v. linkLine Communications, Inc.* (2009) that "the market for high-speed Internet service is now quite competitive" and that "DSL providers face stiff competition from cable companies and wireless and satellite providers."

These judicial and regulatory precedents discredit any claims that *Turner's* bottleneck rationale justifies curtailing Internet providers' editorial discretion more than newspapers'. Absent such justification, the print model dictates that Internet providers' editorial discretion represents a major, if not the dominant, consideration in the free-speech calculus.

Implications

As the forgoing discussion shows, in a world of mass-media content, some degree of intermediation is unavoidable. Individual end users cannot be expected to sift through the avalanche of content available on the Internet by themselves. Instead, they will inevitably turn to some actor exercising editorial discretion to help them organize and manage the ever-growing barrage of information. The proper question, then, is not *whether* such a relationship will develop but, rather, with *whom* it will develop.

Not only is intermediation inevitable. The Supreme Court has repeatedly recognized that the editorial discretion exercised by intermediaries serves important free-speech values. Indeed, the phrases "absolute freedom" and "virtually insurmountable barrier" attest to the importance this function plays in promoting free speech. Although the Supreme Court has recognized a handful of exceptions to this principle, it has already held two of those exceptions inapplicable to the Internet and entered findings in other cases that make it unlikely the third exception will apply.

In so holding, the Court did not ignore the possibility that such an intermediary might screen out certain viewpoints. In the words of the Court in *CBS v. DNC* (1973), "For better or worse, editing is what editors are for; and editing is selection and choice of material." To prevent editors from playing this role would dissipate much of their value. More importantly, the Court recognized that government intervention to limit so-called private censorship would pose far greater dangers, threatening our country's well established free-speech tradition.

There is thus a certain irony implicit in calling on government intervention to limit editorial discretion in the name of preserving free speech. Moreover, claims that an intermediary's decisions have hurt a particular party should be approached with some skepticism. By their nature, exercises of editorial discretion inevitably favor some speakers over others. Indeed, that is the entire point. The flip side is that any intermediary exercise of editorial discretion inevitably pleases some and upsets others. The claims of those disappointed by these outcomes ought not to receive too much weight, lest we risk foreclosing the free-speech benefits that flow from an intermediary's help sorting out the flood of content on the Internet. Furthermore, we risk attributing the gravity of a constitutional dispute to a mere garden-variety disagreement over the quality of particular content.

10

Incomplete Convergence
and the Myth of the One Screen

For nearly two decades, debates about Internet policy have been framed by a convergent vision of the future in which all major forms of communications are all available through a single platform.[20] Industry observers often look forward to the day when they can terminate their other network relationships and simply purchase a single connection capable of providing them with voice, video, text, data, and all of their other communications services. That said, a world of complete convergence has a dark side. End users who are completely dependent on a single provider for all their network services are vulnerable to anticompetitive and opportunistic practices. In addition, this vision implicitly assumes that every application and piece of content must be available through every pipe.

I believe that the case for complete convergence is overstated. The most casual perusal of end users' actual usage patterns reveals numerous reasons for maintaining multiple connections—to provide backup in case of network failure, to enhance network performance, and to allow the end user to enjoy the benefits of different functionalities that particular technologies perform better than others. These considerations are sufficiently compelling to lead most consumers to multihome—that is, maintain multiple network connections—rather than place all of their faith in a single network connection.

In fact, the forces impelling end users away from single homing suggests that the vision in which end users receive all of their communications services through a single screen may well be unobtainable in the

---

[20] For a prominent early mention, see Kapor 1991.

end. This in turn relieves policymakers from having to ensure that any single connection represents everything to everyone. Instead, it permits a more robust environment in which different network providers are free to experiment with different bundles of services and content.

Reliability, Network Performance, and Cost Reduction

Many end users maintain multiple connections to ensure that they always have network access, should one network fail. As an initial matter, most corporate customers multihome to provide back-up protection against the potential breakdown of their primary network connection. It bears mentioning that end users multihoming to protect themselves against system failure must make sure that both connections they are purchasing are truly independent, or they may be dismayed to find that a single accident—say, a backhoe accidentally cutting through the conduit—causes both services to fail.

Multihoming also provides protection against network problems that fall short of complete system failure. For example, secondary connections can serve as safety valves for overflow traffic during periods of peak utilization when spikes in traffic saturate all of the capacity available on the primary network. The most sophisticated load balancing systems can even use the presence of multiple connections to improve network performance by testing both connections and allocating the traffic that is more time sensitive to the link that is running faster.

In addition, load balancers can use the presence of multiple connections to manage and lower network costs. As noted in chapter 8, many industry actors connect to the network through transit charges, which resemble the pricing regimes that currently dominate mobile-phone pricing. Those connecting to the network via transit pricing must prepay a flat rate for a fixed amount of bandwidth (known as the *committed rate*). If their usage exceeds that amount, they must pay incremental amounts based on a usage scale. An end user who pays this type of usage-sensitive pricing can minimize the total network cost by allocating traffic so as to use all of the bandwidth for which they have already paid under their committed rate before incurring any incremental charges.

Moreover, the existence of multiple connections can also reduce total network cost by making sure that network traffic complies with the restrictions imposed by backbone peering. As noted earlier, peering agreements typically require that traffic passing in both directions be roughly equal, insisting that these two flows remain within a ratio of 1.5 to 1 or 2 to 1. A network that has too much traffic passing in one direction can avoid incurring the financial penalties of violating their peering agreements (including the eventual sanction of having the peering agreement cancelled altogether) by redirecting some of the excess traffic through its secondary network. Forcing some of its overflow traffic to travel along a longer path than it would normally would be offset by the network's reduction in cost as a whole.

Differences in Technological Capability and Services

Another consideration that leads end users to maintain more than one network connection is the difference in functional capabilities among transmission technologies. The most obvious difference is the support for mobility provided by wireless connections. The high value that end users place on mobility provides a strong incentive for them to maintain at least one wireless connection. At the same time, the fact that wireless connections are subject to strict bandwidth limitations provides strong incentives for end users to maintain wireline connections as well. The result is that many, if not most, end users opt to maintain both wireless and wireline connections rather than relying exclusively on one platform or the other.

Moreover, some technologies do a better job than others at supporting specific applications. For example, although spectrum-based technologies are relatively ineffective when it comes to highly interactive, bandwidth-intensive applications—such as videoconferencing, graphics-oriented online games like World of Warcraft, and virtual worlds—they can be very effective at transmitting the type of static video content associated with traditional broadcast and cable television. Indeed, a single direct broadcast satellite (DBS) channel provided by DirecTV or EchoStar can distribute programming to the entire Western Hemisphere.

Variations in performance may mean content and applications will migrate to different platforms based on each platform's relative technological strengths and weaknesses. Indeed, platforms may become so specialized that they will be more appropriately regarded as complements rather than substitutes, with network providers maintaining multiple technologies and dynamically routing traffic along particular transmission technologies depending on the nature of the traffic (Yoo 2003).

Furthermore, as discussed in chapter 5, the increasing heterogeneity of what end users are demanding from the network is changing the natural level of standardization in the network. If what end users want from the network is uniform, the optimal solution is to provide a single network designed to deliver exactly what they want. As end user expectations diversify, network services ought to diversify as well, creating what I have elsewhere called *network diversity*, so as to benefit both individual end users and society as a whole (Yoo 2006).

These technological and service-oriented differences provide a powerful impetus for end users to maintain multiple connections, as so doing allows them to take advantage of the different functional capabilities of each transmission technology. End users whose demands are relatively broad or intense are likely to subscribe to more than one service, as demonstrated by increasing numbers of avid televisions fans who subscribe to both cable television and DBS. The increase in the heterogeneity of end users' preferences and the intensity of the demands they are placing on the network since the mid-1990s make this outcome more and more likely with each passing year.

Implications

The likelihood that end users will maintain more than one network connection has important implications for broadband policy. As an initial matter, the fact that end users will likely have multiple connections makes it less important that every possible source be available from every possible connection. A multihomed end user unable to access particular content or applications through a primary connection is not harmed if access through a secondary connection is available. In short, every connection need not be everything to every end user. Instead, end users will continue to enjoy the benefits associated with the Internet so long as they can obtain access through one of their connections.

Equally important, multihoming places a sharp limit on the ability of any particular last-mile provider to engage in anticompetitive activity. The presence of alternatives induces price competition that moderates the prices that any network provider can charge. Moreover, multihoming provides a safety valve that curbs network participants' ability and incentive to engage in strategic behavior that harms consumers. The availability of an alternative channel inherently limits the scope of network providers' ability to raise price, degrade quality, or deny access, as an alternative path for traffic already exists. This in turn weakens the bargaining position of network providers, which is equivalent to reducing their market shares (Besen et al. 2001).

By preventing markets with network economic effects from devolving into winner-take-all markets, multihoming also has the effect of counteracting the tipping and lock-in effects often associated with network economic effects. The same conclusion is reinforced by the literature discussing how adapters or converters (which effectively give consumers access to multiple networks in the same way that multihoming does) affect competition. The presence of perfect, low-cost adapters that can serve as gateways between two networks essentially eliminates any anticompetitive concerns. To the extent that adapters are imperfect, their impact on social welfare is ambiguous, as they may either benefit or harm consumers (Katz and Shapiro 1985; Farrell and Saloner 1992).

Lastly, the literature on two-sided markets shows how multihoming benefits consumers. For example, multihoming generally reduces prices, as the availability of substitutes is generally associated with greater competition (Rochet and Tirole 2003). Multihoming can also offset the effects of otherwise problematic practices. For example, if a two-sided market is composed of a single-homed side and a multihomed side, the former can extract rents from the latter. Such concerns disappear if both sides of the market are multihomed (Evans 2003; Armstrong 2006; Armstrong and Wright 2007). In addition, exclusivity arrangements, tying, and other strategic partnerships can promote consumer welfare when both sides of the market are multihomed (Choi 2010).

In short, the fact that consumers are likely to maintain multiple connections enhances competition, which in turn benefits consumers. At the same time, multihoming also obviates the need for every connection to be everything to everyone.

11

The Maturation of the Industry

Among the many fundamental changes the Internet has undergone over the past fifteen-plus years is the transition of its economic environment. When the Internet was an emerging technology, growth came primarily from attracting new customers who were not already in the market. Over time the Internet matured and began to approach market saturation. Economists and management scholars have long explored this transition—how an industry emerges from its initial high-growth phase and moves into its more mature phases, and how this alters the nature of competition. Their theories suggest that many of the very changes to the Internet's architecture that have concerned many observers may in fact simply be part of the natural evolution of any maturing industry (see, generally, Decherney, Ensmenger, and Yoo forthcoming; Yoo 2010c).

Supply-Side Theories

Nobel Prize winner George Stigler offered one of the earliest and best-known theories describing how the nature of competition and industry structure change over time (1951). He argued that vertical integration in an industry follows a U shape—vertically integrated in the beginning, transitioning to vertically disintegrated during maturity, and then returning once again to vertically integrated as it declines. Because young industries often employ new materials and technologies typically unavailable on the open market, these industries must initially produce all of their key inputs themselves. As demand for their product is established, production grows sufficiently large, and risk drops to the point where third parties have strong incentives to begin providing these inputs. But as the industry enters its decline phase, the drop-off in sales volume means these same third-party input providers disappear, and the industry must once again provide these inputs for itself. Since Stigler first published his theory in 1951, a literature has emerged that empirically assesses his life cycle theory of vertical integration.[21]

Many eminent scholars have identified similar patterns in media industries. Ithiel de Sola Pool (1983, p. 35) notes that during the first generation of radio stations, "broadcasters themselves had to take responsibility for putting on programs." And the history of the cable industry provides a particularly dramatic demonstration of this dynamic.

In 1990, 50 percent of all cable networks and 87 percent of the fifteen most viewed cable networks were vertically integrated. By 2009, these numbers had dropped precipitously; only 6 percent of all cable networks and 13 percent of the fifteen most viewed cable networks were vertically integrated (Yoo 2002 and 2010a). Witnessing this decline, Bruce Owen and Gregory Rosston (2006) and Alfred Kahn (2006a) recanted earlier calls to subject cable television to common-carriage regulation, as the lack of a content industry large enough to support multiple programming streams meant that the cable operators had to finance the initial generation of cable content.[22]

Stigler's observation is also prominently illustrated by Apple Inc., which relied on its proprietary software provider Claris to produce the first generation of software for the Macintosh. Indeed, industries that require the simultaneous development of complementary products often rely on a single, vertically integrated player to get both sides on board (Caillaud and Jullien 2003; Rochet and Tirole 2003).

In 1975, James Utterback and William Abernathy theorized a different supply-side approach, known as *dominant design theory*. They suggested that over time industries will follow the opposite pattern of vertical integration than the one Stigler predicted. Their theory is that every technological breakthrough is followed by a period of initial uncertainty

---

[21] For empirical studies validating Stigler's theory, see Tucker and Wilder 1977, Levy 1984, and Mac-Donald 1985. For empirical studies drawing the contrary conclusion, see Etgar 1978, Stuckey 1983, Harrigan 1985, Wright and Thompson 1986, and Demsetz 1988.

[22] For their initial support for regulating cable operators as common carriers, see Owen (1970) and Kahn (1971, 35–43).

as to which product features will most appeal to consumers and which technologies will most effectively deliver those features. This uncertainty discourages specialization in production and advantages flexible production processes. Later, once the product standardizes around a dominant design, the nature of competition changes: Standardization of the product makes any further major changes prohibitively costly; and at the same time, the firm deploys increasingly specialized equipment in an attempt to increase efficiency and lower costs.

Many scholars initially assumed that once a dominant design had emerged, the desire for greater control over production processes would lead to greater vertical integration (Utterback 1994). But later, scholars recognized that industries could accomplish the same objectives through contracts establishing long-term partnerships with suppliers and distributors instead of through formal vertical integration (Utterback and Suárez 1993). This pattern continues until a major change in technology, demand, or government regulation causes the market to undergo *dematurity*, at which point the cycle begins once again (Abernathy and Clark 1985).

Other scholars have refined the analysis still further, suggesting that the life cycle is more likely to be restarted by innovations that destroy the know-how embodied in the existing technological paradigm and that challenge the linkages between the existing paradigm's core technological concepts (Tushman and Anderson 1986; Henderson and Clark 1990). As was the case with Stigler's theory, the empirical literature testing Utterback and Abernathy's dominant design theory is somewhat mixed.[23]

Dominant design theory also has implications for the nature of innovation. Once a market matures, industries tend to become locked into "technological guideposts" or "technological paradigms" that create a "technological trajectory" that limits the way the industry approaches technical problems (Sahal 1981; Dosi 1982). Others contend that the emergence of a dominant design causes the "era of ferment" launched by the innovation to give way to an "era of incremental change" during which "[t]he focus of competition shifts from high performance to lower cost

---

[23] For a survey finding strong empirical support for dominant design theory, see Suarez 2004 and Murmann and Frenken 2006. For empirical studies finding deviations from dominant design theory, see Christensen 1992; Henderson 1995; Klepper 1997; de Bresson and Townsend 1981, and Adner and Levinthal 2001.

and to differentiation via minor design variations and strategic positioning tactics." Once entrenched, the dominant design becomes difficult to dislodge, in part because of the realization of scale economies and learning by doing and in part because social structures—such as operating procedures, organizational power structures, and institutional frameworks—tend to reinforce the status quo (Anderson and Tushman 1990).

These problems are exacerbated if the innovation is part of a web of interdependent technological processes. This web of processes can create a "design hierarchy," in which the overall production process is divided into smaller components, each of which is controlled by different firms. The existence of a design hierarchy has the inevitable effect of facilitating certain types of innovation and discouraging others. Specifically, the design hierarchy encourages innovation that is consistent with the hierarchy while discouraging innovations that deviate from the existing structure (Clark 1985; Henderson and Clark 1990).

These theories raise the concern that the bigger danger may come not from attempts to deviate from the existing architecture, as many in the current policy debate suggest. Instead, it is possible that the maturation of the market can cause the industry to become locked into an obsolete technology. Indeed, as noted in the introduction to this book, a growing number of engineering scholars have raised precisely this concern. That is why, in an attempt to agitate the status quo and find a way to transition to a different network architecture, the federal government has sponsored numerous initiatives, including DARPA's New Architecture (NewArch) project and the National Science Foundation's Global Environment for Network Innovations (GENI) and their Future Internet Design (FIND).

Demand-Side Theories

Other theories explaining industry competition and structure examine how the demand side influences the nature of competition over time. For example, Clayton Christensen, Matt Verlinden, and George Westerman (2002) offer a demand-driven explanation as to why an industry might move over time from vertical integration to vertical disintegration. During an industry's early stages, firms compete by offering greater product functionality. At that time, the interdependency of production functions, the need to stay at the cutting edge of the technological frontier, and the need for unstructured technical dialogue leads them to prefer vertically integrated firm structures. Eventually, market leaders push the level of product improvement past what customers can utilize, at which point the basis for competition shifts to other factors, such as speed to market and customization. This represents a different type of competition, which favors the more vertically disintegrated structure associated with modularity. Like Stigler, however, these scholars see the industry once again returning to vertical integration after the benefits provided by these alternative dimensions have been exhausted and price competition once again refocuses firms on the cost minimization. Unlike Stigler's theory, which turned on specialization of production, the mechanism driving the level of vertical integration under this theory is consumers' ability to absorb the pace of product innovation.

Other scholars have advanced a product life cycle theory that suggests industries will become more vertically integrated as they pass through a series of phases (see Levitt 1965 for the seminal work). During the introduction phase, when producers are focusing on convincing a small number of technically sophisticated early adopters to try the product, little attention is paid to price or product quality. The transition from the introductory phase into the growth phase leads firms to focus on inducing new customers not already in the market to enter. The arrival of the maturity phase causes the nature of competition to change yet again, as future revenue growth depends not on attracting new customers but on delivering greater value to customers who are already in the market, which is achieved by offering more innovative pricing and more specialized services, which in turn requires increasingly specialized equipment. Although the pattern of sales growth predicted by product life cycle theory is the most common, empirical research indicates that other patterns exist as well, which leads some to question the theory's generality.[24]

---

[24] For reviews of the empirical literature confirming the existence of the pattern predicted by product life cycle theory, see Doyle 1976 and Onkvisit and Shaw 1989. For surveys finding other patterns, see Rink and Swan 1979, Tellis and Crawford 1981, and Kotler and Keller 2009.

Transaction Cost Considerations

Stigler's model also drew criticism from Nobel Prize winner Oliver Williamson (1975), who suggested that vertical integration was more the result of firms' attempts to protect themselves against opportunistic behavior than scale economies. Consistent with this insight, David Teece (1986) developed a theory of industry life cycles that combines transaction cost considerations with dominant design theory. Most innovations are not stand-alone products; instead they usually must be combined with other inputs in order to become marketable to consumers. During an industry's initial stages, when firms are struggling to identify the optimal product design, control of these other inputs does not play a significant role. Once the dominant design has emerged, however, the innovator's success turns as much on its bargaining power vis-à-vis the providers of these other inputs as it does on the value provided by its own contributions. If the innovator has to make relationship-specific investments, it will be vulnerable to ex post opportunistic behavior by the providers of these other inputs. The classic solution to this problem is to use long-term contracts to enter into a strategic partnership or, if the costs of external contracting and monitoring exceed the costs of internal governance, through vertical integration. This perspective suggests that the growing use of strategic partnerships may be nothing more than a natural part of a market's evolution after it matures. Thus, Teece concludes that strategic partnerships "ought to be seen not as attempts to stifle competition, but as mechanisms for lowering entry requirements for innovators" (1986, p. 302).

Implications for Business Strategies and Internet Policy

The implications of market maturation theory for business strategies and Internet policy are myriad. The transformation of the Internet from an experimental test bed into a mass-market platform has made major architectural change more difficult, just as design hierarchy theory would predict. The flattening of the adoption curve depicted in chapter 1 inevitably gives network providers incentive to experiment with increasingly specialized equipment, both to lower costs and to deliver higher value to existing customers by offering services tailored for particular subgroups of customers. The desire to provide greater value to customers is creating greater interest in facilitating content providers' longstanding interest in monetizing content. At the same time, rather than pursuing new customers, market maturation is causing firms to deploy increasingly varied pricing schemes to increase the revenue from the existing customer base.

Such strategic partnerships are becoming increasingly common in the Internet. Perhaps the most salient recent example is Apple's decision to make the iPhone available exclusively on the AT&T wireless broadband network. Network providers have also given particular search engines preferred treatment, such as SBC's (now AT&T's) 2001 alliance with Yahoo!, Google's $500 million deal to serve as the default search engine on Clearwire's new wireless broadband network, and Google's recent efforts to negotiate a deal to become the default search engine for the Verizon Wireless broadband network, only to be outbid by Microsoft at the eleventh hour.

The conflicting theoretical results also suggest that policymakers should be careful not to lock the Internet into any particular architecture, and not to reflexively regard deviations from the status quo as inherently anticompetitive. Such measures would reinforce the obstacles to architectural innovation that already exist. Instead, policymakers ought to focus on creating regulatory structures that preserve industry participants' freedom to tussle with new solutions and adapt to changing market conditions. Any other approach risks precluding the industry from following its natural evolutionary path and rendering insuperable the obstacles to architectural innovation that already exist. Even if it is not always possible to precisely anticipate how the nature of competition and innovation will change, that both will change over time is a given. The real question is not *if* the nature of competition and innovation will change but, rather, *how* and *when*.

Conclusion

When trying to determine how to promote innovation and economic growth, there is a natural tendency to draw guidance from those approaches that have worked in the past. That said, as financial counselors constantly warn us, past results do not guarantee future success. In particular, before reflexively continuing existing regimes, policymakers must carefully consider whether circumstances have changed to the point where a new approach has become necessary.

This is particularly important with a technology such as the Internet, which has undergone such tremendous change over the past fifteen years. What began in the mid-1990s as a means for academics to share e-mail and files through telephone lines now spans a vast number and diversity of end users, applications, technologies, and business relationships. Given the changes in technology and the demands being placed on the network, it is only natural that the industry's architecture and practices would evolve in response.

The importance of basing policy on the future instead of the past is well illustrated if examined through the lens of what has been perhaps the most hotly contested issue in Internet policy over the past five years: network neutrality. The Federal Communications Commission framed its Open Internet proceeding in largely historical terms, arguing the importance of preserving the architecture that had made the Internet so successful in the past (FCC 2009 and 2010). But once the changes that are transforming the Internet have been properly taken into account, practices that initially appeared problematic may turn out to be nothing more than the network's natural attempt to satisfy increasingly varied and complex consumer demand.

Consider first the role of standardization, which the FCC discusses almost exclusively in laudatory terms. As discussed in chapter 5, however, standardization inevitably involves a tradeoff: On the one hand, it allows all those who adopt the standard to enjoy the benefits of having a large number of other people using the same product, which both lowers costs and increases the value of the network. On the other hand, it inevitably reduces product variety, which in turn forces some end users to forgo some alternative version better suited to their preferences. The optimal tradeoff between these two countervailing considerations largely depends on the heterogeneity of demand. If everyone wants the same thing from the network, the reduction of variety does not hurt end users, and the optimal outcome is to provide a single network optimized for the features that everyone wants. The balance begins to change, however, as end-user preferences become more heterogeneous. As what people want from the network becomes more varied, rather than continuing to see all network providers offering a uniform set of services, one would expect different network providers to begin to diversify the services they offer in an effort to meet these demands. In the extreme case, some end users' needs may be so specialized that they deploy their own network, in which case claims of convergence will be incomplete.

In addition, the increasing diversification of network users should lead the Internet to abandon the relatively informal mode of governance of its early days in favor of more formal mechanisms. As noted earlier, one of the Internet's main advantages is its decentralization, which is what makes it so robust and allows innovation to occur in many different parts of the network simultaneously. As is the case with all features that create benefits, decentralization does come with some drawbacks: The localized nature of decision making in the Internet dictates that no actor is in a position to observe and process all of the information necessary to manage the overall network properly, and independent decisions sometimes aggregate to create outcomes that make sense locally but are detrimental to the network as a whole. Moreover, the lack of a centralized enforcement mechanism to ensure that no actor can behave selfishly, seizing a disproportionate share of network resources, means that network participants have had to rely on informal sanctions to ensure the cooperation of others. But as we saw in chapter 6, such solutions work best in close-knit communities, and the growth in the size and the heterogeneity of market actors has caused this system of informal governance to begin to break down and has created a demand for actors who can organize resources across the entire network to optimize performance, align incentives, and prevent interference by third parties. Then, as noted in chapter 9, these actors can also serve as content intermediaries in a position to help end users sift through the avalanche of content that inundates them every day.

On a related note, policymakers should expect certain functions to shift from the end users operating at the edge into the core of the network. As noted in chapter 7, edge-based solutions are poorly suited to functions such as security and congestion management, which require information about the patterns of traffic being generated by multiple end users. Actors in the core of the network are often better situated to observe the breadth of information needed to perform these functions properly. In addition, new developments like cloud computing take advantage of scale economies in network operations as well as the reduction in variability from aggregating demand that can only take place by shifting functions that used to be performed by hosts into data centers. Thus, although the FCC cited end-user control as one of the touchstones for reasonable discrimination and network management (FCC 2010, pp. 17944–45), it must take care not to apply this consideration in a way that prevents these functions from shifting to their natural locus.

The greater variety of networking and device technologies and the more intensive demands placed by modern applications necessarily complicate management practices and business relationships over time. The most common experiment in Internet management practices is with bandwidth tiers, under which end users pay different amounts based on the capacity they expect to consume in a month, a practice that the FCC has explicitly recognized as permissible (FCC 2010, p. 17945). As noted in chapter 8, however, monthly bandwidth caps constitute relatively imprecise mechanisms for inducing end users to minimize the adverse impact they are imposing on other end users. If high-volume users restrict their activity to off-peak times, they may exceed their bandwidth cap without causing any congestion. Conversely, low-volume users may nonetheless be the source of significant problems if they use the network at the time it is bearing its greatest burdens. The ability to manage networks is further complicated by the limits of an end user's ability to accept prices that change dynamically, which may in turn lead network providers to base pricing on proxies that are correlated with high network usage (Yoo 2006). In addition, the advertising-driven nature of the Internet implicates the economic literature on two-sided markets. Although the FCC expressed skepticism about two-sided markets because they are theoretically ambiguous (FCC 2010, p. 17921, n.80), this reasoning implicitly recognizes that circumstances exist in which more complex pricing on different sides may create benefits for end users and that the FCC should remain open to permitting such practices as it learns more about the empirical foundations.

The changes taking place in the Internet would also lead one to expect industry participants to experiment with different ways of doing business. The need to control costs and coordinate multiple levels of production may lead some firms to enter into strategic partnerships or, if the costs of negotiating and enforcing long-term contracts get too high, to vertically integrate. It is possible that the entire industry may shift to such practices. It is also possible that such structural changes may make sense only for certain firms. As a result, we ought not to expect that every industry participant will follow the same institutional form. Any such expectation would contradict the insights for which Ronald Coase, Elinor Ostrom, and Oliver Williamson won their Nobel Prizes.

More generally, though, the Internet's first decade and a half in the public spotlight offers many lessons. As an initial matter, the changes in end users, applications, technologies, and business relationships suggest that the corresponding solutions will vary across technologies and particular locations. They are almost certain to vary over time, as market demand and the underlying cost structure make different alternatives more or less attractive.

Indeed, network engineering is inherently an exercise in tradeoffs that does not lend itself to broad generalizations. There is no such thing as a perfect, inherently superior architecture. Instead, the optimal architecture for any particular network depends on the nature of the flows passing through the network as well as the costs of the technologies comprising the network. This perspective stands in stark contrast to the categorical tone that has dominated debates over Internet policy for the past five years.

The shifts in the technological and economic environment surrounding the network should remind everyone involved in Internet policy of the importance of embracing change. Although new pricing policies, network-management techniques, strategic partnerships, and business models can be quite disruptive, such change is an essential part of technological progress and remains a key sign of an industry's innovative health. Any attempt to foreclose particular practices risks blocking the industry from following its natural evolutionary path.

In addition, differences in technology will doubtlessly demand different types of responses in different portions of the network. As a result, policymakers should refrain from offering one-size-fits-all solutions. Instead, they should adopt flexible policies that give innovation the breathing room it needs. Although governance must remain flexible, the increase in the number of network participants and the erosion of trust dictate that governance also become more formal. Perhaps the best means for creating such an environment is to create a regulatory-enforcement regime that evaluates any charges of improper behavior on a case-by-case basis after the fact, as I have long advocated. So long as the burden of proof is placed on the party challenging the practice, such a regime should provide sufficient breathing room for industry participants to experiment with new solutions for emerging problems while simultaneously safeguarding consumers against any anticompetitive practices.

Rather than engaging in prescriptive regulatory oversight, the government would better serve us by promoting competition in other ways, such as by reducing switching costs for consumers, lowering entry barriers by new producers, and increasing transparency in business relationships. Such steps would benefit consumers while simultaneously permitting industry actors to try out different responses to growing problems. It would also avoid putting the government in the position of locking the industry into any particular conception of the network's architecture. Such a tack would appropriately and humbly reflect our ability to foresee how the network is likely to evolve in the future.

References

Abernathy, William J., and Kim B. Clark. 1985. Innovation: Mapping the winds of creative destruction. *Research Policy* 14: 3–22.

Abernathy, William J., and James M. Utterback. 1978. Patterns of industrial innovation. *Technology Review* 80 (7): 40–47.

Adner, Ron, and Daniel Levinthal. 2001. Demand heterogeneity and technology evolution: Implications for product and process innovation. *Management Science* 47 (5): 611–28.

Anderson, Philip, and Michael L. Tushman. 1990. Technological discontinuities and dominant designs: A cyclical model of technological change. *Administrative Science Quarterly* 35 (4): 604–33.

Anderson, Thomas, Larry Peterson, Scott Shenker, and Jonathan Turner. 2005. Overcoming the Internet impasse through virtualization. *Computer* 38 (4): 34–41.

Arkansas Educational Television Commission v. Forbes, 523 U.S. 666 (1998).

Armstrong, Mark. 2006. Competition in two-sided markets. *RAND Journal of Economics* 37 (3): 668–91.

Armstrong, Mark, and Julian Wright. 2007. Two-sided markets, competitive bottlenecks and exclusive contracts. *Economic Theory* 32 (2): 353–80.

Arthur, W. Brian. 1989. Competing technologies, increasing returns, and lock-in by historical events. *Economic Journal* 99 (394): 116–31.

Ashcroft v. ACLU, 542 U.S. 656, 667 (2004).

Banniza, Thomas-Rolf, Dietrich Boettle, Ralf Klotsche, Peter Schefczik, Michael Soellner, and Klaus Wuenstel. 2009. A European approach to a clean slate design for the future Internet. *Bell Labs Technical Journal* 14 (2): 5–22.

Barlow, John P. 1996. A declaration of the independence of cyberspace. http://homes.eff.org/~barlow/Declaration-Final.html.

Baumol, William J., and David F. Bradford. 1970. Optimal departures from marginal cost pricing. *American Economic Review* 60 (3): 265–83.

Bellovin, Steven M., David D. Clark, Adrian Perrig, and Dawn Song. 2005. A clean slate design for the next-generation secure Internet. Report for NSF Global Environment for Network Innovations (GENI) Workshop, July 12–14, 2005. http://sparrow.ece.cmu.edu/group/pub/bellovin_clark_perrig_song_next GenInternet.pdf.

Benjamin, Robert, and Rolf Wigand. 1995. Electronic markets and virtual value chains on the information superhighway. *Sloan Management Review* 36 (2): 62–72.

Berglas, Eitan. 1976. On the theory of clubs. *American Economic Review: Papers and Proceedings of the Eighty-Eighth Annual Meeting of the American Economic Association* 66 (2): 116–21.

Berman, Jerry, and Daniel J. Weitzner. 1995. Abundance and user control: Renewing the democratic heart of the First Amendment in the age of interactive media. *Yale Law Journal* 104 (7): 1619–37.

Besen, Stanley, Paul Milgrom, Bridger Mitchell, and Padmanabhan Srinagesh. 2001. Advances in routing technologies and Internet peering agreements. *American Economic Review: Papers and Proceedings of the Hundred Thirteenth Annual Meeting of the American Economic Association* 91 (2): 292–96.

Blake, Steven, David L. Black, Mark A. Carlson, Elwyn Davies, Zheng Wang, and Walter Weiss. 1998. *An architecture for differentiated services.* Internet Engineering Task Force Network Working Group, Request for Comments 2475. http://www.rfc-archive.org/getrfc.php?rfc=2475.

Blumenthal, Marjory S., and David D. Clark. 2001. Rethinking the design of the Internet: The end-to-end arguments vs. the brave new world. *ACM Transactions on Internet Technology* 1 (1): 70–109.

Borland, John. 2006. Net video explosion triggers traffic jam worries. *CNET News* February 23. http://news.cnet.com/Net-video-explosion-triggers-traffic-jam-worries/2100-1025_3-6042300.html.

Braden, Bob, David D. Clark, Jon Crowcroft, Bruce Davie, Steve Deering, Deborah Estrin, Sally Floyd, Van Jacobson, Greg Minshall, Craig Partridge, Larry Peterson, K. K. Ramakrishnan, Scott Shenker, John Wroclawski, and Lixia Zhang. 1998. *Recommendations on queue management and congestion avoidance in the Internet.* Internet Engineering Task Force Network Working Group, Request for Comments 2309. http://www.rfc-archive.org/getrfc. php?rfc=2309.

Braden, Bob, David Clark, and Scott Shenker. 1994. *Integrated services in the Internet architecture: An overview.* Internet Engineering Task Force Network Working Group, Request for Comments 1633. http://www.rfc-archive.org/getrfc.php?rfc=1633.

Bradner, Scott. 1999. The Internet Engineering Task Force. In *Open sources: Voices from the open source revolution*, ed. Chris DiBona, Sam Ockman, and Mark Stone, 47–52. Sebastopol, Calif.: O'Reilly.

————. 2006. The end of end-to-end security? *IEEE Security and Privacy* 4 (2): 76–79.

Braun, Hans-Werner. 1995. *NSFNET: The National Science Foundation Network.* http://hpwren.ucsd.edu/~hwb/NSFNET/NSFNET_Hist/.

Bresnahan, Timothy. 1999. New modes of competition: Implications for the future structure of the computer industry. In *Competition, innovation, and the Microsoft monopoly: Antitrust in the digital marketplace*, ed. Thomas Lenard and Jeffrey Eisenach, 155–208. Boston: Kluwer Academic Publishers.

Brodkin, Jon. 2010. Amazon cloud uses FedEx instead of the Internet to ship data. *Network World*, June 10. http://www.networkworld.com/news/2010/061010-amazon-cloud-fedex.html.

Caillaud, Bernard, and Bruno Jullien. 2003. Chicken & egg: Competition among intermediation service providers. *RAND Journal of Economics* 34 (2): 309–28.

Canon, Scott. 2009. Metered Internet likely on way. *Seattle Times*, May 11. http://seattletimes.nwsource.com/html/businesstechnology/2009204491_btisps11.html.

Canter, Laurence A., and Martha S. Siegel. 1994. *How to make a fortune on the information superhighway: Everyone's guerrilla guide to marketing on the Internet and other on-line services*. New York: Harper Collins.

Carmi, Shai, Shlomo Havlin, Scott Kirkpatrick, Yuval Shavitt, and Eran Shir. 2007. A model of Internet topology using k-shell decomposition. *Proceedings of the National Academy of Sciences of the United States of America* 104 (27): 11150–54.

Carpenter, Brian. 1996. *Architectural principles of the Internet*. Internet Engineering Task Force Network Working Group, Request for Comments 1958. http://www.rfc-archive.org/getrfc.php?rfc=1958.

Carr, Nicholas. 2008. *The big switch: Rewiring the world, from Edison to Google*. New York: W.W. Norton & Co.

CBS, Inc. v. FCC, 453 U.S. 367 (1981).

Choi, Jay Pil. 2010. Tying in two-sided markets with multi-homing. *Journal of Industrial Economics* 58 (3): 607–26.

Christensen, Clayton M. 1992. Exploring the limits of the technology S-curve. *Production & Operations Management* 1 (4): 334–57.

Christensen, Clayton M., Matt Verlinden, and George Westerman. 2002. Disruption, disintegration, and the dissipation of differentiability. *Industrial and Corporate Change* (5) 11: 955–93.

Cisco Systems, Inc. 2007. *Cisco visual networking index: Forecast and methodology, 2006–2011*.

———. 2008a. *Approaching the zettabyte era*. White paper. http://www.cisco.com/en/US/solutions/collateral/ns341/ns525/ns537/ns705/ns827/white_paper_c11-481374_ns827_Networking_Solutions_White_Paper.html.

———. 2008b. *Cisco visual networking index: Forecast and methodology, 2007–2012*. http://www.nextgenweb.org/wp-content/uploads/2008/06/cisco-visual-networking-index-white-paper.pdf.

———. 2009. *Cisco visual networking index: Forecast and methodology, 2008–2013*. http://www.cisco.com/web/BR/assets/docs/whitepaper_VNI_06_09.pdf.

———. 2010a. *Cisco visual networking index: Forecast and methodology, 2009–2014.*

———. 2010b. *General Cisco visual networking index (VNI) Q&A.*

———. 2011a. *Cisco visual networking index: Global Mobile Data Traffic Forecast Update, 2010–2015.* http://www.cisco.com/en/US/solutions/collateral/ns341/ns525/ns537/ns705/ns827/white_paper_c11-520862.pdf.

———. 2011b. *Cisco visual networking index: Forecast and methodology, 2010–2015.* http://www.cisco.com/en/US/solutions/collateral/ns341/ns525/ns537/ns705/ns827/white_paper_c11-481360.pdf.

City of Los Angeles v. Preferred Communications, Inc., 476 U.S. 488 (1986).

Clark, David D. 1988. The design philosophy of the DARPA Internet protocols. *ACM SIGCOMM Computer Communication Review* 18 (4): 106–14.

———. 1992. A cloudy crystal ball: Visions of the future. In *Proceedings of the twenty-fourth Internet Engineering Task Force*, ed. Megan Davies, Cynthia Clark, and Debra Legare, 540–43. Reston, Va.: Corporation for National Research Initiatives. http://www.ietf.org/proceedings/prior29/IETF24.pdf.

———. 2008. *Written statement of Dr. David Clark.* En banc hearing on broadband network management practices. Written statement. http://www.fcc.gov/broadband_network_management/022508/clark.pdf.

Clark, David D., and Marjory S. Blumenthal. 2011. The end-to-end argument and application design: The role of trust. *Federal Communications Law Journal* 63 (2): 357–90.

Clark, David D., Bill Lehr, Steve Bauer, Peyman Faratin, and Rahul Sami. 2006. Overlay networks and the future of the Internet. *Communications and Strategies* 63 (3): 1–21.

Clark, David D., Karen Sollins, John Wroclawski, Dina Katabi, Joanna Kulik, Xiaowei Yang, Robert Braden, Ted Faber, Aaron Falk, Venkata Pingali, Mark Handley, and Noel Chiappa. 2003. *New arch: Future generation Internet architecture.* Final report. http://www.isi.edu/newarch/iDOCS/final.finalreport.pdf.

Clark, David D., John Wroclawski, Karen R. Sollins, and Robert Braden. 2005. Tussle in cyberspace: Defining tomorrow's Internet. *IEEE/ACM Transactions on Networking* 13 (3): 462–75.

Clark, Kim B. 1985. The interaction of design hierarchies and market concepts in technological evolution. *Research Policy* 14 (5): 235–51.

Clinton, William J. 1996. Remarks in Knoxville, Tennessee. *Public papers of the president.* Vol. 2. October 10.

Coase, Ronald H. 1946. The marginal cost controversy. *Economica* 13 (51): 169–82.

———. 1972. Industrial organization: A proposal for research. In *Policy issues and research opportunities in industrial organization.* Vol. 3 of *Economic research: Retrospect and prospects*, ed. Victor Fuchs, 59–73. New York: National Bureau of Economic Research.

Columbia Broadcasting System, Inc. v. Democratic National Committee, 412 U.S. 94 (1973).

Comcast Cablevision of Broward County, Inc. v. Broward County, 124 F. Supp. 2d 685 (S.D. Fla. 2000).

Comer, Douglas. 2006. *Internetworking with TCP/IP*. Upper Saddle River, N.J.: Pearson Prentice Hall.

Cotter, Thomas F. 2006. Some observations on the law and economics of intermediaries. *Michigan State Law Review* 2006 (1): 67–82.

Crowcroft, Jon. 2007. Net neutrality: The technical side of the debate: A white paper. *ACM SIGCOMM Computer Communication Review* 37 (1): 49–55.

Crowcroft, Jon, and Peter Key. 2007. Report from the Clean Slate Network research post-SIGCOMM 2006 workshop. *ACM SIGCOMM Computer Communication Review* 37 (1): 75–78.

David, Paul A. 1985. Clio and the economics of QWERTY. *American Economic Review: Papers and Proceedings of the Ninety-Seventh Annual Meeting of the American Economic Association* 75 (2): 332–37.

de Bresson, C., and J. Townsend. 1981. Multivariate models for innovation: Looking at the Abernathy-Utterback model with other data. *Omega: The International Journal of Management* 9 (4): 429–36.

Decherney, Peter, Nathan Ensmenger, and Christopher S. Yoo. 2001. Are those who ignore history doomed to repeat it? *University of Chicago Law Review* 78 (4): 1627–85.

Delaney, Kevin, and Bobby White. 2007. Video surge divides Web watchers. *Wall Street Journal*. August 14, B1.

Demsetz, Harold. 1988. Vertical integration: Theories and evidence. In *Ownership, control, and the firm: The organization of economic activity*. Vol. 1, ed. Harold Demsetz, 166–86. Oxford, UK, and New York: Basil Blackwell.

Denver Area Educational Telecommunications Consortium v. FCC, 518 U.S. 727 (1996).

Dosi, Giovanni. 1982. Technological paradigms and technological trajectories: A suggested interpretation of the determinants and directions of technological change. *Research Policy* 11 (3): 147–62.

Dovrolis, Constantine. 2008. What would Darwin think about clean-slate architectures? *ACM SIGCOMM Computer Communication Review* 38 (1): 29–34.

Downes, Larry, and Chunka Mui. 1998. *Unleashing the killer app: Digital strategies for market dominance*. Boston: Harvard Business School Press.

Downs, David. 2008. BitTorrent, Comcast, EFF antipathetic to FCC regulation of P2P traffic. *S.F. Weekly*. 23 January.

Doyle, Peter. 1976. The realities of the product life cycle. *Quarterly Review of Marketing* 1 (Summer): 1–6.

Economides, Nicholas. 2008. "Net neutrality," nondiscrimination, and digital distribution of content through the Internet. *I/S: A Journal of Law and Policy for the Information Society* 4 (2): 209–33.

Ellacoya Networks, Inc. 2007. *Ellacoya* data shows Web traffic overtakes peer-to-peer (P2P) as largest percentage of bandwidth on the network. Press release. http://www.businesswire.com/news/home/20070618005912/en/Ellacoya-Data-Shows-Web-Traffic-Overtakes-Peer-to-Peer .

Ellickson, Robert. 1991. *Order without law: How neighbors settle disputes.* Cambridge, Mass., and London, UK: Harvard University Press.

Ellison, Larry. 2009. Oracle CEO Larry Ellison bashes "cloud computing" hype. ForaTv. http://www.youtube.com/watch?v=UOEFXaWHppE.

Etgar, Michael. 1977. A test of the Stigler theorem. *Industrial Organization Review* 5 (2 & 3): 135–37.

European Commission. n.d. *FIRE: Future Internet and experimentation.* http://cordis.europa.eu/fp7/ict/fire/home_en.html.

European Commission Directorate-General for the Information Society. 2010. *Internet development across the ages.* European Commission Directorate-General for the Information Society and Project SMART 2008/0049. http://cordis.europa.eu/fp7/ict/fire/docs/executive-summary_en.pdf.

Evans, David S. 2003. The antitrust economics of multisided markets. *Yale Journal on Regulation* 20 (2): 325–81.

Faratin, Peyman, David Clark, Steven Bauer, William Lehr, Patrick Gilmore, and Arthur Berger. 2008. The growing complexity of Internet interconnection. *Communications & Strategies* 1 (72): 51–72.

Farrell, Joseph, and Paul Klemperer. 2007. Coordination and lock-in: Competition with switching costs and network effects. In *Handbook of industrial organization,* ed. Mark Armstrong and Robert H. Porter, 1967–2072. Vol. 3. Amsterdam; London: North-Holland.

Farrell, Joseph, and Garth Saloner. 1985. Standardization, compatibility, and innovation. *RAND Journal of Economics* 16 (1): 70–83.

―――. 1986a. Installed base and compatibility: Innovation, product pre-announcements, and predation. *American Economic Review* 76 (5): 940–55.

―――. 1986b. Standardization and variety. *Economics Letters* 20 (1): 71–74.

―――. 1992. Converters, compatibility, and the control of interfaces. *Journal of Industrial Economics* 40 (1): 9–35.

FCC v. League of Women Voters of California, 468 U.S. 364 (1984).

FCC v. Midwest Video Corp., 440 U.S. 689 (1979).

FCC v. Pacifica Foundation, 438 U.S. 726 (1978).

Federal Communications Commission (FCC). 2007. *High-speed services for Internet access: Status as of December 31, 2006.* http://hraunfoss.fcc.gov/edocs_ public/attachmatch/DOC-277784A1.pdf.

―――. 2009. Preserving the open Internet, notice of proposed rulemaking. *Federal Communications Commission Record* 24 (15) 13064–127.

―――. 2010. Preserving the open Internet, report and order. *Federal Communications Commission Record* 25 (21): 17905–18098.

————. 2011a. Implementation of Section 6002(b) of the Omnibus Budget Reconciliation Act of 1993, fifteenth report. *Federal Communications Commission Record* 26 (12): 9664–9971.

————. 2011b. *Internet access services: Status as of December 31, 2010.* http://hraunfoss.fcc.gov/edocs_public/attachmatch/DOC-310261A1.pdf.

Feist, Sharael. 2002. Newsmaker: The father of modern spam speaks. *CNET News.* 26 March. http://news.cnet.com/2008-1082-868483.html.

Feldmann, Anja. 2007. Internet clean-slate design: What and why? *ACM SIG-COMM Computer Communication Review* 37 (3): 59–64.

Floyd, Sally, and Kevin Fall. 1999. Promoting the use of end-to-end congestion control in the Internet. *IEEE/ACM Transactions on Networking* 7 (4): 458–72.

Gill, Phillipa, Martin Arlitt, Zongpeng Li, and Anirban Mahanti. 2008. The flattening Internet topology: Natural evolution, unsightly barnacles or contrived collapse? In *Passive and active network management: 9th international conference, PAM 2008,* ed. Mark Claypool and Steve Uhlig, 1–10. Berlin and Heidelberg, Germany: Springer Verlag.

Greenstein, Shane. 2010. Glimmers and signs of innovative health in the commercial Internet. *Journal on Telecommunications and High Technology Law* 8 (1): 25–78.

Gupta, Piyush, and P. R. Kumar. 2000. The capacity of wireless networks. *IEEE Transactions on Information Theory* 46 (2): 388–404.

Handley, Mark. 2006. Why the Internet only just works. *BT Technology Journal* 24 (3): 119–29.

Hansell, Saul. 2008. A smart bet or a big mistake? *New York Times.* 19 August.

Harrigan, Kathryn Rudie. 1985. Vertical integration and corporate strategy. *Academy of Management Journal* 28 (2): 397–425.

Henderson, Rebecca. 1995. Of life cycles real and imaginary: The unexpectedly long old age of optical lithography. *Research Policy* 24 (4): 631–43.

Henderson, Rebecca M., and Kim B. Clark. 1990. Architectural innovation: The reconfiguration of existing product technologies and the failure of established firms. *Administrative Science Quarterly* 35 (1): 9–30.

Hetcher, Steven A. 2001. Norm proselytizers create a privacy entitlement in cyberspace. *Berkeley Technology Law Journal* 16 (2): 877–935.

Hoffman, Paul, and Susan Harris. 2006. *The Tao of IETF: A novice's guide to the Internet Engineering Task Force.* Internet Engineering Task Force Network Working Group, Request for Comments 4677. http://www.rfc-archive.org/getrfc.php?rfc=4677.

Houle, Joseph, K. K. Ramakrishnan, Rita Sadhvani, Murat Yuksel, and Shiv Kalyanaraman. 2007. *The evolving Internet: Traffic, engineering, and roles.* Paper presented at the 35th annual Telecommunications Policy Research Conference. http://www.cse.unr.edu/~yuksem/my-papers/2007-tprc.pdf.

ICANN. n.d. *ICANN factsheet.* http://www.icann.org/en/factsheets/fact-sheet.html.

International Center for Advanced Internet Research. 2010. *Grand challenges in advanced networking research.* http://www.icair.org/mission/grand-challenges.html.

International Telecommunication Union. n.d. *ICT statistics database.* http://www.itu.int/ITU-D/ICTEYE/Indicators/Indicators.aspx.

Internet Systems Consortium. 2011. *The ISC domain survey.* https://www.isc.org/solutions/survey/.

Internet World Stats. 2010. *United States of America: Internet usage and broadband usage report.* http://www.internetworldstats.com/am/us.htm.

Jackson, Charles. 2011. Wireless efficiency versus net neutrality. *Federal Communications Law Journal* 63 (2): 445–80.

Jacobson, Van. 1988. Congestion avoidance and control. *ACM SIGCOMM Computer Communication Review* 18 (4): 314–29.

Johnson, David R., and David Post. 1996. Law and borders: The rise of law in cyberspace. *Stanford Law Review* 48 (5): 1367–402.

Kahn, Alfred E. 1971. *The economics of regulation: Principles and institutions.* Vol. 2. New York: Wiley & Sons.

———. 2006a. *A Democratic voice of caution on net neutrality, Progress Snapshot, release 2.24.* http://www.pff.org/issues-pubs/ps/2006/ps2.24voiceofcautiononnetneutrality.html.

———. 2006b. Telecommunications: The transition from regulation to antitrust. *Journal on Telecommunications and High Technology Law* 5 (1): 159–88.

Kapor, Mitchell. 1991. Testimony before the Subcommittee on Telecommunications and Finance of the House Committee on Energy and Commerce. 102d Congress, October 24.

Katz, Michael L., and Carl Shapiro. 1985. Network externalities, competition, and compatibility. *American Economic Review* 75 (3): 424–40.

———. 1992. Product introduction with network externalities. *Journal of Industrial Economics* 40 (1): 55–83.

———. 1994. Systems competition and network effects. *Journal of Economic Perspectives* 8 (2): 93–115.

Kempf, James, and Rob Austein. 2004. *The rise of the middle and the future of end-to-end: Reflections on the evolution of the Internet architecture.* Internet Engineering Task Force Network Working Group, Request for Comments 3724. http://www.rfc-archive.org/getrfc.php?rfc=3724.

Kende, Michael. 2000. *The digital handshake: Connecting Internet backbones.* Working paper no. 32, FCC Office of Plans and Policy. http://www.fcc.gov/Bureaus/OPP/working_papers/oppwp32.pdf.

Kim, Ryan. 2008. Online bandwidth hogs to be cut off at trough? All-you-can-eat Internet days may be over as providers test limits, metered pricing. *San Francisco Chronicle.* 23 June. http://articles.sfgate.com/2008-06-23/business/17165424_1_time-warner-cable-users-bandwidth-hogs.

Klepper, Steven. 1997. Industry life cycles. *Industrial and Corporate Change* 6 (1): 145–81.

Kolodny, Lara, and Georg Szalai. 2006. Verizon facing uphill FiOS battle. *Hollywood Reporter*. 27 March.

Kotler, Philip, and Kevin Lane Keller. 2009. *Marketing management*. 13th ed. Upper Saddle River, N.J.: Pearson Prentice Hall.

Kurose, James F., and Keith W. Ross. 2010. *Computer networking: A top-down approach*. Boston: Addison-Wesley.

Laffont, Jean-Jacques, and Jean Tirole. 2000. *Competition in telecommunications*. Cambridge, Mass.: MIT Press.

Laskowski, Paul, and John Chuang. 2009. *A leap of faith? From large-scale testbed to the global Internet*. Unpublished manuscript presented at TPRC's 37th Research Conference on Communication, Information, and Internet Policy. September 27. http://www.tprcweb.com/images/stories/papers/Laskowski_2009.pdf.

Leathers v. Medlock, 499 U.S. 439 (1991).

Leland, Will, Murad S. Taqqu, Walter Willinger, and Daniel V Wilson. 1994. On the self-similar nature of ethernet traffic (extended version). *IEEE/ACM Transactions on Networking* 2 (1): 1–15.

Lemley, Mark. 1998. The law and economics of Internet norms. *Chicago-Kent Law Review* 73 (4): 1257–94.

Lessig, Lawrence. 2001. *The future of ideas*. New York: Random House.

————. 2006. Net neutrality: Hearing before the Senate Committee on Commerce, Science, and Transportation. 109th Congress, 2nd session, February 7. http://commerce.senate.gov/public/?a=Files.Serve&File_id=c5bf9e54-b51f-4162-ab92-d8a6958a33f8.

Levitt, Theodore. 1965. Exploit the product life cycle. *Harvard Business Review* 43 (6): 81–94.

Levy, David. 1984. Testing Stigler's interpretation of "The division of labor is limited by the extent of the market." *Journal of Industrial Economics* 32 (3): 377–89.

Levy, Steven. 2008. Pay per gig. *Washington Post*. 30 January. http://www.washingtonpost.com/wp-dyn/content/article/2008/01/29/AR2008012903205.html.

Lewis, Peter. 1994. An ad (gasp!) in cyberspace. *New York Times*. 19 April. http://www.nytimes.com/1994/04/19/business/an-ad-gasp-in-cyberspace.html.

Liebowitz, Stan J., and Stephen E. Margolis. 1996. Should technology choice be a concern of antitrust policy? *Harvard Journal of Law & Technology* 9 (2): 283–318.

Lipsey, Richard G., Peter O. Steiner, and Douglas D. Purvis. 1987. *Economics*. 8th ed. New York: Harper and Row.

Liu, Joseph P. 1999. Legitimacy and authority in Internet coordination: A domain name case study. *Indiana Law Journal* 74 (2): 587–626.

MacDonald, James M. 1985. Market exchange or vertical integration: An empirical analysis. *Review of Economics and Statistics* 67 (2): 327–31.

Malone, Thomas W., Joanne Yates, and Robert I. Benjamin. 1987. Electronic markets and electronic hierarchies. *Communications of the ACM* 30 (6): 484–97.

Markoff, John, and Saul Hansell. 2006. Hiding in plain sight, Google seeks an expansion of power. *New York Times*. 14 June.

Martin, James, and James Westall. 2007. Assessing the impact of BitTorrent on DOCSIS networks. In *Proceedings of the fourth international Conference on Broadband Communications, Networks, Systems (BroadNets)*, 423–32. http://ieeexplore.ieee.org/stamp/stamp.jsp?tp=&arnumber=4550464.

Martin, Olivier. 2007. State of the Internet and challenges ahead. Working paper, ICTC Consulting. http://www.ictconsulting.ch/reports/NEC2007-OH Martin.doc.

Mathis, Matt, and Bob Briscoe. 2011. *Congestion exposure (ConEx): Concepts and abstract mechanism*. Internet Engineering Task Force congestion exposure working group, Internet draft. http://datatracker.ietf.org/doc/draft-ietf-conex-abstract-mech/.

Mehta, Stephanie. 2006. Behold the server farm! Glorious temple of the information age! *Fortune*. 7 August.

Merit Network, Inc. 1996. *NSFNET: A partnership for high-speed networking; final report, 1987–1995*. http://www.merit.edu/documents/pdf/nsfnet/nsfnet_report.pdf.

Miami Herald Publishing Co. v. Tornillo, 418 U.S. 241 (1974).

Minar, Nelson, and Marc Hedlund. 1999. A network of peers: Peer-to-peer models through the history of the Internet. In *Peer-to-peer: Harnessing the benefits of a disruptive technology*, ed. Andy Oram, 3–20. Sebastopol, Calif.: O'Reilly & Associates.

Minnesota Internet Traffic Studies. n.d. *Internet growth trends and Moore's Law*. http://www.dtc.umn.edu/mints/igrowth.html.

———. 2009. *MINTS pages updated, many new reports, further slight slowdown in wireline traffic growth rate*. http://www.dtc.umn.edu/mints/news/news_22.html.

Mitchell, Bridger M. 1978. Optimal pricing of local telephone service. *American Economic Review* 68 (4): 517–37.

Mitomo, Hitoshi. 2001. The political economy of pricing: Comparing the efficiency impacts of flat-rate vs. two-part tariffs. *Communications and Strategies* 44: 55–70.

Moffett, Craig. 2006. *Wall Street's perspective on telecommunications: Hearing before the Senate Committee on Commerce, Science, and Transportation*. 109th Congress, March 14. http://commerce.senate.gov/pdf/moffett-031406.pdf.

Mueller, Milton. 2002. *Ruling the root: Internet governance and the taming of cyberspace*. Cambridge, Mass.: MIT Press.

Murmann, Johann Peter, and Koen Frenken. 2006. Toward a systematic framework for research on dominant designs, technological innovations, and industrial change. *Research Policy* 35 (7): 925–52.

Nagle, John. 1985. *On packet switches with infinite storage*. Internet Engineering Task Force Network Working Group, Request for Comments 970. http://www.rfc-archive.org/getrfc.php?rfc=970.

National Science Foundation (NSF). n.d.a. *FIND: NSF NeTS FIND initiative*. http://www.nets-find.net.

———. n.d.b. *Future Internet Architectures (FIA)*. http://www.nsf.gov/funding/pgm_summ.jsp?pims_id=503476.

———. n.d.c. *Global Environment for Network Innovations (GENI)*. http://www.nsf.gov/funding/pgm_summ.jsp?pims_id=501055.

Nemertes Research. 2007. The Internet singularity, delayed: Why limits in Internet capacity will stifle innovation on the Web. http://www.nemertes.com/studies/internet_singularity_delayed_why_limits_internet_capacity_will_stifle_innovation_web (membership required).

Nocera, Joe. 2008. Stuck in Google's doghouse. *New York Times*. 13 September. http://www.nytimes.com/2008/09/13/technology/13nocera.html.

Norton, William. 2006. *Video Internet: The next wave of massive disruption to the U.S. peering ecosystem (v0.91)*. Draft paper. www.pbs.org/cringely/pulpit/media/InternetVideo0.91.pdf .

Odlyzko, Andrew M. 2003. Internet TV: Implications for the long distance network. In *Internet television*, ed. Eli Noam, Jo Groebel, and Darcy Gerbang, 9–18. London, UK, and New York: Routledge.

Onkvisit, Sak, and John J. Shaw. 1989. *Product life cycles and product management*. New York: Quorum Books.

Ortiz, Sixto, Jr. 2008. Internet researchers look to wipe the slate clean. *Computer* 41 (1): 12–16.

Ostrom, Elinor. 1990. *Governing the commons: The evolution of institutions for collective action*. Cambridge, Mass.: Cambridge University Press.

Owen, Bruce M. 1970. Public policy and emerging technology in the media. *Public Policy* 18 (4): 539–52.

Owen, Bruce M., and Gregory L. Rosston. 2006. Local broadband access: *Primum non nocere* or *primum processi*? A property rights approach. In *Net neutrality or net neutering: Should broadband Internet services be regulated?*, ed. Thomas M. Lenard and Randolph J. May, 163–94. New York: Springer.

Pacific Bell Telephone Co. v. linkLine Communications, Inc., 129 S. Ct. 1109 (2009).

Paltridge, Sam. 1998. *Internet traffic exchange: Developments and policy*. Paper, working party on telecommunications and information services policies, OECD. http://www.oecd.org/dataoecd/11/26/2091100.pdf.

Park, Rolla Edward, and Bridger M. Mitchell. 1987. *Optimal peak-load pricing for local telephone calls*. Rand paper, no. R-3404-1-RC. http://www.rand.org/pubs/reports/R3404-1/.

Perl, Lewis. 1985. *Impacts of local measured service in South Central Bell's service area in Kentucky*. Unpublished manuscript, prepared by National Economic Research Associates for South Central Bell Telephone Company.

Pew Internet and American Life Project. n.d. *Trend data: Usage over time.* http://www.pewinternet.org/Trend-Data/Usage-Over-Time.aspx.

Pool, Ithiel de Sola. 1983. *Technologies of freedom.* Cambridge, Mass.: Belknap Press.

Radin, Margaret Jane, and R. Polk Wagner. 1998. The myth of private ordering: Rediscovering legal realism in cyberspace. *Chicago-Kent Law Review* 73 (4): 1295–317.

Ramakrishnan, K. K., Sally Floyd, and David L. Black. 2001. *The addition of explicit congestion notification (ECN) to IP.* Internet Engineering Task Force Network Working Group, Request for Comments 3168. http://www.rfc-archive.org/getrfc.php?rfc=3168.

Ramsey, Frank P. 1927. A contribution to the theory of taxation. *Economic Journal* 37 (145): 47–61.

Ratnasamy, Sylvia, Scott Shenker, and Steven McCanne. 2005. Towards an evolvable Internet architecture. *ACM SIGCOMM Computer Communication Review* 35 (4): 313–24.

Raynovich, R. Scott. 2005. Google's own private Internet. *Light Reading.* 20 September. http://www.lightreading.com/document.asp?doc_id=80968.

Red Herring. 1999. InterNAP wakes up transmission quality. 21 April. http://redherring.com/Home/1744.

Red Lion Broadcasting Co. v. FCC, 395 U.S. 367 (1967).

Reed, David. 2000. *The end of the end-to-end argument.* http://www.reed.com/dpr/locus/Papers/endofendtoend.html.

Reno v. ACLU, 521 U.S. 844 (1997).

Reuters. 2007. Google, cable firms warn of risks from Web TV. *USA Today.* 7 February.

Rink, David R., and John E. Swan. 1979. Product life cycle research: A literature review. *Journal of Business Research* 7 (3): 219–42.

Rochet, Jean-Charles, and Jean Tirole. 2003. Platform competition in two-sided markets. *Journal of the European Economic Association* 1 (4): 990–1029.

Rohlfs, Jeffrey. 1974. A theory of interdependent demand for a communications service. *Bell Journal of Economics and Management Science* 5 (1): 16–37.

Rosen, Eric, Arun Viswanathan, and Ross Callon. 2001. *Multiprotocol label switching architecture.* Internet Engineering Task Force Network Working Group, Request for Comments 3031. http://www.rfc-archive.org/getrfc.php?rfc=3031.

Sahal, Devendra. 1981. *Patterns of technological innovation.* Reading, Mass.: Addison-Wesley.

Saltzer, Jerome. 1999. *"Open access" is just the tip of the iceberg.* http://web.mit.edu/Saltzer/www/publications/openaccess.html.

Saltzer, Jerry H., David P. Reed, and David D. Clark. 1984. End-to-end arguments in system design. *ACM Transactions on Computer Systems* 2 (4): 277–88.

Sandvig, Christian. 2010. *How to see wireless.* Remarks presented at the conference on "Rough Consensus and Running Code: Integrating Engineering Principles into the Internet Policy Debates," Center for Technology, Innovation, and Competition, University of Pennsylvania Law School, Philadelphia.

Sarkar, Mitra Barun, Brian Butler, and Charles Steinfeld. 1995. Intermediaries and cybermediaries: A continuing role for mediating players in the electronic marketplace. *Journal of Computer Mediated Communication* 1 (3). http://jcmc.indiana.edu/vol1/issue3/sarkar.html.

Scherer, F. M., and David Ross. 1990. *Industrial market structure and economic performance*. 3rd ed. Boston: Houghton Mifflin Co.

Scott, Judy. 2000. Emerging patterns from the dynamic capabilities of Internet intermediaries. *Journal of Computer Mediated Communication* 5 (3). http://jcmc.indiana.edu/vol5/issue3/scott.html.

Shalunov, Stanislav, Greg Hazel, Janardhan Iyengar, and Mirja Kuehlewind. 2011. *Low extra delay background transport (LEDBAT)*. Internet Engineering Task Force LEDBAT working group, Internet draft. http://datatracker.ietf.org/doc/draft-ietf-ledbat-congestion/.

Shannon, Claude E. 1948a. A mathematical theory of communication (pt. 1). *Bell Systems Technical Journal* 27 (3): 379–423.

———. 1948b. A mathematical theory of communication (pt. 2). *Bell Systems Technical Journal* 27 (3): 623–56.

Shenker, Scott, David Clark, Deborah Estrin, and Shai Herzog. 1996. Pricing in computer networks: Reshaping the research agenda. *Telecommunications Policy* 20 (3): 183–201.

Spulber, Daniel, and Christopher Yoo. 2005. On the regulation of networks as complex systems: A graph theory approach. *Northwestern University Law Review* 99 (4): 1687–722.

Spyropoulos, Thrasyvoulos, Serge Fdida, and Scott Kirkpatrick. 2007. Future Internet: Fundamentals and measurement. *ACM SIGCOMM Computer Communication Review* 37 (2): 101–6.

Stanford University Clean Slate Project. n.d. *Program goals*. http://cleanslate.stanford.edu/index.php.

Stigler, George. 1951. The division of labor is limited by the extent of the market. *Journal of Political Economy* 59 (3): 185–93.

Stuckey, J. A. 1983. *Vertical integration and joint ventures in the aluminum industry*. Cambridge, Mass.: Harvard University Press.

Suárez, Fernando F. 2004. Battles for technological dominance: An integrative framework. *Research Policy* 33 (2): 271–86.

Swanson, Brett. 2007. The coming exaflood. *Wall Street Journal*. 20 February.

Swanson, Brett, and George Gilder. 2008. *Estimating the exaflood: The impact of video and rich media on the Internet; a "zettabyte" by 2015?* Paper, Discovery Institute. http://www.discovery.org/scripts/viewDB/filesDB-download.php?command=download&id=1475.

Tanenbaum, A. 2003. *Computer networks*. 4th ed. Upper Saddle River, N.J.: Prentice Hall.

Teece, David J. 1986. Profiting from technological innovation: Implications for integration, collaboration, licensing and public policy. *Research Policy* 15 (6): 285–305.

TeleGeography Research. 2007. *Global Internet geography*. Washington, D.C.: PriMetrica, Inc.

———. 2008. *Global Internet geography*. Washington, D.C.: PriMetrica, Inc.

———. 2009. *Global Internet geography*. Washington, D.C.: PriMetrica, Inc.

———. 2010. *Global Internet geography*. Washington, D.C.: PriMetrica, Inc.

———. 2011. *Global Internet geography*. Washington, D.C.: PriMetrica, Inc.

Tellis, Gerald J., and C. Merle Crawford. 1981. An evolutionary approach to product growth theory. *Journal of Marketing* 45 (4): 125–32.

Train, Kenneth. 1994. *Optimal regulation*. Cambridge, Mass.: MIT Press.

Tucker, Irvin B., and Ronald P. Wilder. 1977. Trends in vertical integration in the U.S. manufacturing sector. *Journal of Industrial Economics* 26 (1): 81–94.

Turner Broadcasting System, Inc. v. FCC, 512 U.S. 622 (1994).

Tushman, Michael L., and Philip Anderson. 1986. Technological discontinuities and organizational environments. *Administrative Science Quarterly* 31 (3): 439–65.

United States Telecom Association v. FCC, 290 F.3d 415 (D.C. Cir.) (2002).

Utterback, James M. 1994. *Mastering the dynamics of innovation: How companies can seize opportunities in the face of technological change*. Boston, Mass.: Harvard Business School Press.

Utterback, James M., and William J. Abernathy. 1975. A dynamic model of process and product innovation. *Omega: The International Journal of Management Science* 3 (6): 639–56.

Utterback, James M., and Fernando F. Suárez. 1993. Innovation, competition, and industry structure. *Research Policy* 22 (1): 1–21.

Vance, Ashlee. 2009. In the new data center, it's roofs off and taxes down. *New York Times*. 17 August. http://bits.blogs.nytimes.com/2009/08/17/in-the-new-data-center-its-roofs-off-and-taxes-down/.

van Schewick, Barbara. 2010. *Internet architecture and innovation*. Cambridge, Mass.: MIT Press.

Viscusi, W. Kip, Joseph E. Harrington Jr., and John M. Vernon. 2005. *Economics of regulation and antitrust*. 4th ed. Cambridge, Mass.: MIT Press.

Volokh, Eugene. 1995. Cheap speech and what it will do. *Yale Law Journal* 104 (7): 1805–50.

Vorhaus, David. 2007. *Confronting the albatross of P2P*. Boston: Yankee Group.

Weinberg, Jonathan. 2000. ICANN and the problem of legitimacy. *Duke Law Journal* 50 (1): 187–260.

Weinman, Joe. 2011. As time goes by: The law of cloud response time. http://www.joeweinman.com/Resources/Joe_Weinman_As_Time_Goes_By.pdf.

Welch, Creighton A. 2009. Big Internet usage could cost you big bucks. *San Antonio Express-News*. 2 April.

Williamson, Oliver E. 1975. *Markets and hierarchies: Analysis and antitrust implications.* New York: Free Press.

Windhausen Jr., John. 2008. *A blueprint for big broadband.* EDUCAUSE white paper. http://www.educause.edu/ir/library/pdf/EPO0801.pdf.

Wright, Mike, and Steve Thompson. 1986. Vertical disintegration and the life-cycle of firms and industries. *Managerial and Decision Economics* 7 (2): 141–44.

Yoo, Christopher S. 2002. Vertical integration and media regulation in the new economy. *Yale Journal on Regulation* 19 (1): 171–300.

———. 2003. The rise and demise of the technology-specific approach to the First Amendment. *Georgetown Law Journal* 91 (2): 245–356.

———. 2004. Would mandating broadband network neutrality help or hurt competition? A comment on the end-to-end debate. *Journal on Telecommunications and High Technology Law* 3 (1): 23–68.

———. 2005. Beyond network neutrality. *Harvard Journal of Law & Technology* 19: 1–77.

———. 2006. Network neutrality and the economics of congestion. *Georgetown Law Journal* 94 (6): 1847–908.

———. 2008. Network neutrality, consumers, and innovation. *University of Chicago Legal Forum* (2008): 169–262.

———. 2009. Network neutrality after *Comcast*: Toward a case-by-case approach to reasonable network management. In *New directions in communications policy*, ed. Randolph May, 55–83. Durham, N.C.: Carolina Academic Press.

———. 2010a. Comments before the Federal Communications Commission, applications of Comcast Corp., General Electric Co., and NBC Universal, Inc., for consent to assign licenses and transfer control of licenses. http://fjallfoss.fcc.gov/ecfs/document/view?id=7020472619.

———. 2010b. Free speech and the myth of the Internet as an unintermediated experience. *George Washington Law Review* 78 (4): 697–773.

———. 2010c. Innovations in the Internet's architecture that challenge the status quo. *Journal on Telecommunications and High Technology Law* 8 (1): 79–99.

———. 2011. Technologies of control and the future of the First Amendment. *William and Mary Law Review* 53 (2): 747–775.

Zhao, Jinjing, Peidong Zhu, Xicheng Lu, and Lei Xuan. 2008. Does the average path length grow in the Internet? In *Information networking: Towards ubiquitous networking and services*, ed. Teresa Vazão, Mário M. Freire, and Ilyoung Chong, 183–90. Berlin and Heidelberg, Germany: Springer Verlag.

Zittrain, Jonathan. 1999. ICANN: Between the public and the private. *Berkeley Technology Law Journal* 14 (3): 1071–93.

Index

About the Author

Christopher S. Yoo is the John H. Chestnut Professor of Law, Communication, and Computer & Information Science and the Founding Director of the Center for Technology, Innovation and Competition at the University of Pennsylvania. He has emerged as one of the nation's leading authorities on law and technology. His research focuses on how the principles of network engineering and the economics of imperfect competition can provide insights into the regulation of the Internet and other forms of electronic communications. He has been a leading voice in the "network neutrality" debate that has dominated Internet policy for the past several years and has testified frequently before Congress, the Federal Communications Commission, the Federal Trade Commission, and foreign regulatory authorities. He is also pursuing research on copyright theory as well as the history of presidential power. Before entering the academy, Professor Yoo clerked for Justice Anthony M. Kennedy of the Supreme Court of the United States and Judge A. Raymon Randolph of the U.S. Court of Appeals for the D.C. Circuit. He also practiced law with Hogan & Hartson under the supervision of now-Chief Justice John G. Roberts, Jr. He is a graduate of Harvard College, the Anderson School at the University of California, Los Angeles, and the Northwestern University School of Law.